# VEGAN
# SANDWICHES
# SAVE THE DAY!

# VEGAN SANDWICHES SAVE THE DAY!

## REVOLUTIONARY NEW TAKES ON EVERYONE'S FAVORITE ANYTIME MEAL

### CELINE STEEN and TAMASIN NOYES

FAIR WINDS
PRESS
BEVERLY, MASSACHUSETTS

◄ *Torta de Tofu*, page 141

© 2012 Fair Winds Press
Text © 2012 Tamasin Noyes and Celine Steen
Photography © 2012 Fair Winds Press

First published in the USA in 2012 by
Fair Winds Press, a member of
Quayside Publishing Group
100 Cummings Center, Suite 406-L
Beverly, MA 01915-6101
www.fairwindspress.com

16 15 14 13 12     1 2 3 4 5

ISBN: 978-1-59233-525-1

Digital edition published in 2012
eISBN: 978-1-61058-030

Library of Congress Cataloging-in-Publication
Data available

Book and cover design by Debbie Berne Design
Photography by Celine Steen

Printed and bound in China

With heartfelt appreciation,
we share our sandwiches
with all who take steps to improve
the well-being of animals.
Thank you for striving for
safe and peaceful lives
for all on this planet.

# CONTENTS

# INTRODUCTION:
# THE BEST THING TO HAPPEN TO SLICED BREAD

If you're like 99 percent of the people we know, including ourselves, we're ready to wager that sandwiches are as important to your eating life as they are to ours.

Maybe it's because they bring forth fond childhood memories, such as picnics with family and friends, or because they're the edible solace that sustains many of us when we find ourselves flooded with work. And what's not to like about them? They're portable, affordable, and easy, and they make a healthy option for lunch, dinner, or even breakfast. They also present us with endless possibilities as far as the type of bread, filling, and preparation go, so everyone can be happy.

In these pages, vegans and nonvegans alike will find endless eats to tickle their fancy, from pressed sandwiches to open-faced delights, burgers, wraps, and even dessert sandwiches.

Where some people see bread, we see opportunity, as well as another chance to play with textures and flavors. Sure, you might need forks and knives for a few of these, but sometimes the best things just can't be contained.

When it comes to these sandwich creations, the world is our stage. All it takes is one quick glance at the incredible variety that abounds—Vietnam and its *bánh mì*, India and its *pav bhaji*, France and its *pan bagnat*—to realize that slapping tasty stuff between a couple of slices of bread is one of the greatest culinary delights on the planet.

So grab your brown paper bag, and join us on this trip to supreme "sandwich-hood." We can't wait to get started!

◀ *Something Blackened*
*This Way Comes*, page 118

# CHAPTER ONE

## SANDWICHING MADE EASY

**TIPS AND TRICKS TO MAKE YOUR SANDWICH-BUILDING EXPERIENCE A BREEZE**

Some cookbooks have you follow the instructions they contain to the letter, but we're not sticklers for rules. We want you to look at our recipes and let your imagination run wild.

**FOR EXAMPLE:** You have a favorite bread you'd rather use instead of the one we recommend? Go for it! You eat gluten- or soy-free foods for medical reasons or just because you prefer it that way? We absolutely understand and encourage you to follow your heart, needs, and taste buds.

It's obvious that most breads vary in size, and while our recipes are correct for what we used, subbing in a different type might give you a smaller or larger yield than ours, so plan accordingly.

We like to alternate between using whole grain breads and plainer ones, and this part is entirely up to you: If you prefer using whole grain all the time, rest assured our recipes will work just as well for you. On the other hand, if you're more of a white bread kind of person, that's just fine by us, too.

We are also A-OK with the fact that not everyone has the time or inclination to make everything from scratch, be it bread or cold cuts. We won't think any less of you if you choose to purchase these items from your favorite store instead of using the recipes herein. Just remember to check the label for nonvegan ingredients, as they have this annoying habit of showing up in the most unexpected places.

Want to shake things up even more? Go nuts by picking a filling you like from one of our recipes and seeing how it works with a different spread, wrapper, bunch of veggies, or preparation . . . the possibilities are close to endless.

## TIPS FOR SANDWICHING ON THE GO

It's undeniable: we're all super-busy people, so chances are we're going to have to take our sandwiches on the road sometimes, and no one wants to look forward to lunch only to come face to face with a soggy, sad excuse for a sandwich.

We also all want to make sure that our sandwiches remain as safe to eat as when we prepared them in the morning, especially when the high summer temperatures are relentless. Here are few nifty tips that will help keep such sandwiching nightmares at bay.

- Place thick lettuce leaves, spinach, or any such barrier-like leafy vegetable on the bread, and then add the spread. This will keep the moisture of the spread away from the bread. Let's give it up for all-powerful lettuce leaves, willing to take one for the team! Just be sure to thoroughly spin your washed lettuce leaves dry, not only to keep them fresh and robust for a longer period but also to prevent them from being the culprit in bread soakage.

- Lightly toast your bread to make it a little more resistant to moist fillings. Be sure to let it cool a little if you're going to apply lettuce leaves directly to it so the residual heat doesn't make the lettuce wilt.

- When we're dealing with super-moist fillings like cabana cheese (page 53) and want to prepare the sandwiches ahead of time, we prefer skipping soft sandwich bread for a crustier one like ciabatta or baguette, which will absorb the flavors, but not the moisture.

- Many of us saw our mothers or caretakers spread a thin layer of butter on the inside of our sandwiches, a move that wasn't done solely to impart flavor to the sandwich, but also to form a barrier against unwanted sogginess. Nondairy butter will do the trick beautifully for our proud vegan sandwiches.

- Keep your lunchbox cool by freezing a (freezable) bottle of water or juice overnight and placing it next to your carefully wrapped (think waterproof!) sandwiches so that by the time your lunch break rolls around, the water bottle will have thawed while at the same time keeping your food items cool.

- Another excellent solution, and probably our favorite of the bunch because we both suffer from tremendous sogginess-phobia, is to pack all the sandwich components separately in reusable, eco-friendly, airtight containers that you'll bring back home to clean at the end of the day (lucky you!), so that the sandwiches can be assembled right at the time they're going to be eaten. This is especially recommended for sandwiches that are most susceptible to becoming soggy. If you have children, you'll find that they are very likely to love this idea because it allows them to play with their food and build their sandwiches according to their own rules.

- Some sandwiches can be made travel-friendly by just wrapping them very snugly in foil to hold the filling tightly. That is the case for the Country Sausage Sandwiches (page 19), Tempeh Arugula Caesar Wraps (page 68), and Muffaletta (page 122), to name but a few.

## BUT WAIT, THERE'S MORE! (TIPS, THAT IS)

We come bearing a few extra tips to help you get this sandwiching party started.

- If you buy a lot of bread in bulk because the sale is too good to be true (we sure do), but then feel overwhelmed because there's just no way you'll ever eat that much bread while it's in its prime freshness (we plead guilty to that, too), you can safely place it in the freezer in the packaging it came in and thaw it later, toasting it to bring back the crustness if needed. This works for sandwich bread, bagels, you name it.

- Speaking of freshness, there are a few instances when staleness actually comes in handy: that would be the case when making French toast, because stale bread is less likely to fall apart on you when you soak it in the batter. That would also be the case with panini, where a too-soft bread will press down too much and flatten to almost cracker thinness. Using less-fresh bread or thicker bread will yield far better results in this case.

- And while we're on the subject of panini, here's a nifty way to prepare panini without a panini press: heat either a smooth-top grill pan or a large skillet over medium heat. Place the sandwich in the pan. On top of the sandwich, place either a foil-wrapped brick or other similarly heavy object, such as a cast-iron pan. Cook for 2 to 3 minutes or until browned, then carefully repeat the process on the other side. Flat panini weights (larger than sandwich size, with a handle) are also available in cooking stores.

## IN OUR KITCHENS: OUR GUIDE TO KEY INGREDIENTS

Here is a condensed list of the possibly less well-known items you're very likely to find at all times in our kitchens. They will make an appearance in at least one or more of our recipes.

CREAMED COCONUT: Creamed coconut is an unsweetened, creamy paste made from the meat of mature coconuts. Unlike regular coconut cream sold in Tetra Paks, creamed coconut needs to be diluted in order to be used as milk or cream.

Our favorite creamed coconut is Let's Do . . . Organic, but we hear great things about the Renuka brand.

We dilute the 7-ounce (198-g) package in 1¾ cups (415 ml) warm water and use it in our recipes to make cheese, sauces, and more. Look for it online, at health food stores, or at ethnic grocery shops in your neighborhood.

**INSTANT TAPIOCA:** In the United States, Minute brand is available in the pudding aisle of grocery stores, while Let's Do . . . Organic is available at health stores and online. When used with vital wheat gluten, it enhances the texture of our cold cuts.

**INSTANT YEAST:** We've used instant yeast throughout this book. The advantage of instant yeast is that it does not need to be proofed before use, but can just be added to the dry ingredients during preparation. It can be stored for 6 months at room temperature or in the fridge, or for over a year in the freezer. While yeast can work well coming straight out of the freezer, it's not the case with every brand out there. Read the instructions on the package, and if nothing is mentioned, remove the amount of yeast you need from the freezer, and let it come back to room temperature before use.

   If you prefer active dry yeast, it is usually recommended to substitute 1 teaspoon instant yeast with 1¼ teaspoons active dry. To proof the yeast, combine it with the amount of warm water the recipe calls for. Add ⅛ teaspoon sugar. The mixture should become bubbly after approximately 10 minutes, which is a sign the yeast is active and good to go.

**JACKFRUIT:** Jackfruit is a starchy fruit that gets lots of attention for its meaty texture. We use the canned variety that comes in brine or water, not in syrup, and shred it to replicate pulled pork. It's available at most Asian grocery shops.

**LIQUID SMOKE:** Actually made from smoke, this is a dark, concentrated liquid. Different companies vary in their preparation, but regardless of how it is manufactured, it brings a woodsy, smoky undertone to the taste profile.

**MACA POWDER:** We use this dried, powdered root parsimoniously and only optionally because it is

expensive, but its slightly cheesy, buttery flavor is great and the fact that it's packed with vitamins, minerals, and amino acids is an added bonus.

**MAYONNAISE:** If you make your own mayo, more power to you! If not, our favorite is Vegenaise Reduced Fat.

**MISO:** Prevalent in Japanese cooking, this fermented paste is made from soybeans or grains and can be added to countless dishes. White or shiro miso is our miso of choice because it is a bit milder than other kinds.

**NONDAIRY MILKS:** We use unsweetened plain nondairy milks (almond is our favorite) because they're the most versatile in the kitchen. A few recipes require soymilk and are listed as such.

**NUTRITIONAL YEAST:** This deactivated yeast is yellow and slightly cheese-like in flavor, and also a powerhouse of B vitamins. Do not confuse it with brewer's yeast.

**SEITAN:** Seitan is made from vital wheat gluten. It's a protein with a terrific texture. We prefer to make our own seitan, but it is also available in well-stocked grocery stores.

**SOY WRAPPERS:** These wraps are just plain fun! Look for them in the ethnic food aisle of the grocery store or order them online. In the United States, they are sold under the name Yamamotoyama. Low in both calories and fat, the wraps are made from soy protein and are also gluten-free. As always, check the label for yourself because ingredients can change.

**TAMARI:** We use the reduced-sodium version of this condiment, which is similar to soy sauce, but thicker and richer in flavor. Wheat-free versions are also available.

**TEMPEH:** This is a cultured soybean product that is sold in cakes. Unlike tofu, which is made from soymilk, tempeh is made from partially cooked soybeans, which gives it a different texture.

**TEXTURIZED VEGETABLE PROTEIN:** Sold in granules or chunks, this dehydrated protein appears in a couple of recipes in this book. It's made from defatted soy flour and adds texture, especially when combined with vital wheat gluten in our meatless balls.

**TOFU:** Made from soymilk, tofu is sold in blocks. We use extra-firm tofu in most recipes, but occasionally you might see firm or silken firm used in specific recipes for different results.

**UME PLUM VINEGAR:** Slightly fruity and salty, this red liquid is a by-product of pickling umeboshi plums. Ume plum is quite pungent, so use it sparingly. It may also reduce your need to add extra salt to recipes. Check the ethnic aisle of your grocery store for it, or substitute red wine vinegar.

**VEGAN WINES:** Wines add acidity to recipes, and also a depth of flavor. They have a tendency to make a dish taste like you put in more effort than you actually did. Feel free to substitute non-alcoholic wines or use our substitution formula, if you prefer. To substitute for red wine, use ½ cup (120 ml) vegetable broth with 2 teaspoons red wine vinegar. For white wine, use ½ cup (120 ml) broth with 2 teaspoons white wine vinegar. For current vegan wine information, email the wineries directly, or check out www.barnivore.com.

**VEGAN WORCESTERSHIRE SAUCE:** Anchovy-free yet full of flavor, the sauce we like best is Wizard brand.

## RECIPE ICONS

Throughout this book you will find recipes labeled in the following way:

 **QUICK & EASY:** Recipes that take under thirty minutes to whip up, provided you have intermediate cooking and/or baking skills.

 **TRAVEL-FRIENDLY:** Recipes that are especially good for transport.

 **POTENTIALLY GLUTEN-FREE:** Recipes that can easily be made gluten-free by swapping store-bought or homemade certified gluten-free ingredients for the ones listed.

We understand how tricky and sometimes frustrating it can be to prepare foods that are not only vegan, but also gluten-free. That's why we really wanted to add substitution suggestions for gluten-free versions in all of our recipes, but because the swaps would have been rather elaborate in some cases, there wasn't enough room to do so.

The simplest and most obvious way to make our sandwiches gluten-free is to pick gluten-free breads or wraps at the store, and to check the labels thoroughly, which you're probably already doing. When in doubt, it's always a wise move to get in touch with the manufacturer directly. Or better yet, if you have the time, make your own gluten-free breads and wraps at home. Unless one of our recipes contains seitan or baked goods, it can be made gluten-free in a snap, as long as you make sure that all the products you use, such as vinegars and mustards, are free of gluten.

When we marked our recipes as having gluten-free potential, we made sure that store-bought gluten-free alternatives were available for the ingredients the recipe calls for and/or that there were gluten-free recipes available on the Internet to make those ingredients at home. As of the printing date, we found gluten-free alternatives for each and every ingredient in our recipes marked as Potentially Gluten-Free.

# CHAPTER TWO

## RISE AND 'WICH

{ **THE EARLY BIRD GETS THE BREAKFAST SANDWICH** }

Sandwiches might not be the first idea to pop into your mind when you sleepily think about your upcoming breakfast, but we've put on our superhero costumes (which are so unforgiving, by the way) and are now officially on a mission to make it so that there's never a wrong time to meet and eat the sandwich of your dreams. Packed with sweet and savory options, this chapter will come to your aid in getting a hands-on head start to your day. Mission accomplished, if we do say so ourselves.

# MEXICAN CHICK-UN AND WAFFLES

Nothing says "Good morning!" like a little spice. We've given a *muy bueno* boost to our version of this breakfast standby. Crispy corn waffles boast seasoned tofu and poblano gravy. Top with chopped tomatoes and avocado, if desired.

| YIELD |
|---|
| 4 SANDWICHES |

**FOR CHICK-UN**

¼ cup (60 ml) dry red wine

1 tablespoon (20 g) minced chipotle in adobo

1 teaspoon ground cumin

1 teaspoon smoked paprika

½ teaspoon dried oregano

½ teaspoon fine sea salt

¼ teaspoon black pepper

1 pound (454 g) extra-firm tofu, drained, pressed, and cut into 8 slices

**FOR WAFFLES AND GRAVY**

1 cup (235 ml) nondairy milk

¾ cup (187 g) fresh or frozen corn, divided

2 tablespoons (28 g) nondairy butter, melted

2 tablespoons (30 ml) canola oil

1 tablespoon (15 ml) pure maple syrup

1 cup (125 g) all-purpose flour

1 tablespoon (15 g) baking powder

½ teaspoon fine sea salt

1 tablespoon (9 g) seeded, minced jalapeño

Nonstick cooking spray

Canola oil, for cooking

1 tablespoon (15 ml) olive oil

1 poblano pepper, cut into half-moons

½ small onion, cut into half-moons

2 cloves garlic, minced

1 cup (235 ml) vegetable broth

1 tablespoon (8 g) cornstarch

Salt and pepper, to taste

**TO MAKE THE CHICK-UN:** Combine the wine, chipotle, and spices in an 8 x 12-inch (20 x 30-cm) pan. Add the tofu, turning to coat. Cover and refrigerate for 1 hour or longer.

**TO MAKE THE WAFFLES:** In a blender, combine the milk, ½ cup (125 g) of the corn, butter, oil, syrup, flour, baking powder, and salt. Blend until smooth. Stir in the remaining ¼ cup (62 g) corn and the jalapeño.

Preheat the oven to 300°F (150°C, or gas mark 2). Cook the waffles according to the waffle iron instructions using nonstick cooking spray. Keep the waffles warm in the oven. You should get 2 standard-size waffles.

Lightly coat a large skillet with canola oil and heat over medium heat. Drain the tofu, reserving any marinade, and cook until brown, about 4 minutes. Cook the other side for about 4 minutes. Keep warm in the oven.

**TO MAKE THE GRAVY:** In the same skillet, combine the olive oil, poblano, and onion. Cook, stirring, for 5 minutes, or until the onions are softened. Add the garlic.

Add the broth and cornstarch to the tofu marinade. Whisk until smooth. Add to the skillet and whisk until thickened, about 3 minutes. Add more chipotle, if desired.

**TO ASSEMBLE THE SANDWICHES:** Break the waffles into quarters. Place a quarter on each plate and top with 2 pieces of tofu and some gravy. Top with the second waffle and tomatoes and avocado.

**SERVING SUGGESTIONS AND VARIATIONS**

Leftover gravy? Hurray! Try it on mashed potatoes.

# COUNTRY SAUSAGE SANDWICHES

As vegans, we love farms! Especially farm sanctuaries. Imagine digging into this all-in-one sandwich as you take in the beautiful country view. Hash browns are a unique addition to a sandwich, but one we think you'll enjoy. Piled with smoky tofu and spinach, this sandwich can be wrapped tightly in foil for easy transporting.

**YIELD**
4 SANDWICHES

## FOR SAUSAGE PATTIES

8 ounces (227 g) tempeh, cut in half widthwise, then lengthwise, to form 4 patties

½ cup (120 ml) vegetable broth

1 tablespoon (15 ml) liquid smoke

1 teaspoon olive oil

1 teaspoon balsamic vinegar

1 tablespoon (6 g) fennel seeds, ground

2 teaspoons smoked paprika

2 teaspoons ground cumin

1 teaspoon ground coriander

1 teaspoon red pepper flakes

1 teaspoon onion powder

1 teaspoon fine sea salt

½ teaspoon black pepper

## FOR SAUCE

¼ cup plus 2 tablespoons (84 g) vegan mayonnaise

2 tablespoons (30 ml) fresh lemon juice

¼ cup plus 2 tablespoons (60 g) minced red onion

¼ cup (38 g) minced red bell pepper

Salt and pepper, to taste

Canola oil, for cooking

## FOR SANDWICHES

1 pound (454 g) frozen hash browns

4 English muffins, split

1 cup (32 g) chopped spinach

**TO MAKE THE SAUSAGE PATTIES:** Simmer the tempeh in boiling water for 20 minutes. In an 8 x 11-inch (20 x 28-cm) pan, combine the broth, liquid smoke, oil, vinegar, and spices. Add the tempeh patties, turning to coat. Refrigerate for 2 hours or more.

After marinating, lightly coat a large skillet with oil and heat over medium heat. Line a plate with a paper towel. Cook the tempeh on one side until browned, 8 to 10 minutes. Cook the other side for 6 to 8 minutes. Transfer the tempeh to the plate.

**TO MAKE THE SAUCE:** Combine all the ingredients in a small bowl. Cover with plastic wrap and refrigerate until ready to use.

**TO ASSEMBLE THE SANDWICHES:** Prepare the hash browns according to the package directions. Using a heaping ½ cup (75 g) of the hash browns, gently form into a round about ½ inch (1.3 cm) thick and the diameter of the English muffin. Repeat so you have 4 rounds.

Preheat a panini press to high. Spread the sauce evenly on the inside of the muffins. Place a tempeh patty on each bottom, then top with the hash browns and ¼ cup (8 g) of the spinach. Put the tops on and place in the panini press. Close the press and cook for 7 to 9 minutes, or until golden brown.

### SERVING SUGGESTIONS AND VARIATIONS

This all-in-one breakfast doesn't really need a side dish, but a cup of fresh fruit always has a place at our tables.

# THE INCREDIBLE GREEN SANDWICH

We went all out and created this monochromatic sandwich as a hybrid of the popular avocado toast and green smoothie recipes everyone seems to be enjoying for breakfast lately.

**YIELD**
8 SANDWICHES

2 small ripe avocados, halved, pitted, and peeled

1 clove garlic, minced (optional)

1½ tablespoons (15 g) minced scallion or 2 teaspoons chopped chives

½ teaspoon minced jalapeño, to taste (optional)

1½ tablespoons (2 g) chopped fresh cilantro or parsley

1½ tablespoons (25 ml) fresh lime juice

Salt, to taste

Fruity extra-virgin olive oil, for drizzling (optional)

8 Green Monster rolls or bagels (see Note), cut in half and toasted

3 cups (100 g) fresh baby spinach

1 ounce (28 g) favorite sprouts (snow pea, alfalfa, etc.)

Mash the avocado with the garlic, scallion, jalapeño, cilantro, lime juice, and salt to taste.

Drizzle a little olive oil on each toasted roll half.

Spread a generous 1 tablespoon (20 g) of guacamole over each roll half.

Top with a handful of spinach and then add a handful of sprouts. Top with the other roll half, and serve.

**RECIPE NOTE**

To make the Green Monster Bread (page 178) into rolls or bagels, begin after the first rise by dividing the deflated dough into 8 equal portions. Shape into rounds by pulling the dough from the sides onto the bottom, or shape into bagels by inserting your thumb in the center of each dough ball, twirling the dough around it until the hole reaches about 1½ inches (3.8 cm) in diameter. Let rest for 15 minutes. Preheat the oven to 375°F (190°C, or gas mark 5).

Combine 8 cups (1.9 L) water and ¼ cup (55 g) baking soda in a large pot. Bring to a boil. Lower the heat to a gentle boil. Add 4 rolls or bagels at a time and simmer for 30 seconds, submerging the rolls or bagels occasionally.

Scoop out the rolls or bagels and drain on a wire rack. Transfer to the prepared baking sheets. Bake for 24 minutes, or until the rolls or bagels sound hollow when tapped. Let cool on a wire rack. Well wrapped, these will freeze just fine, so make them ahead of time for a breakfast that is ready in a snap.

**SERVING SUGGESTIONS AND VARIATIONS**

If you're looking for a protein boost, serve this with your favorite tofu scramble. Make it a pesto tofu scramble to keep the green theme going. Or nosh on a super simple small bowl of warm shelled edamame, sprinkled with a little sea salt.

# OUT FOR THE COUNT OF MONTE CRISTO

French toast bagels? With sauerkraut, for breakfast? It's true, we deviated from what you might think of as a traditional Monte Cristo, but we're betting you'll be glad we did. The savory French toast bagels alone had more than one tester swooning.

## FOR FILLING AND SPREAD

1 tablespoon (15 ml) olive oil

12 ounces (340 g) Moo-Free Seitan (page 180), cut into ½-inch (1.3-cm) strips

1½ cups (210 g) sauerkraut, drained

2 tablespoons (30 g) prepared horseradish, divided

1 tablespoon (15 g) Dijon mustard, divided

¼ teaspoon black pepper

Pinch of red pepper flakes

1 large avocado, peeled and pitted

2 teaspoons fresh lemon juice

## FOR FRENCH TOAST BAGELS

¼ cup (35 g) cashews, soaked in water for 1 hour, then rinsed and drained

½ cup plus 2 tablespoons (150 ml) nondairy milk

2 teaspoons Dijon mustard

1 tablespoon (15 ml) sauerkraut juice

1 tablespoon (15 ml) white wine vinegar

½ teaspoon fine sea salt

⅛ teaspoon black pepper

¼ cup (25 g) minced scallion

1 tablespoon (8 g) all-purpose flour

1 teaspoon baking powder

Canola oil, for cooking

4 bagels, cut in half

**TO MAKE THE FILLING AND SPREAD:** Heat the oil in a large skillet over medium-high heat. Add the seitan strips and cook until seared, 3 to 5 minutes. Add the sauerkraut, 1 tablespoon (15 g) of the horseradish, 1 teaspoon of the mustard and the black pepper and red pepper flakes. Cook, stirring, for 4 minutes. For the spread, place the avocado, lemon juice, remaining 1 tablespoon (15 g) horseradish, and remaining 2 teaspoons mustard in a small bowl. Mash with a fork until smooth.

**TO MAKE THE FRENCH TOAST BAGELS:** Combine the cashews, milk, mustard, sauerkraut juice, vinegar, salt, and pepper in a blender. Process until smooth and then pour into a shallow dish. Stir in the scallion, flour, and baking powder. Heat ⅛ inch (3 mm) of oil in the skillet over medium-high heat. (These are prone to sticking, so add additional oil if needed.) Dip the bagels into the mixture, let the extra batter drip back down into the dish, and transfer to the skillet. Cook for 3 to 4 minutes on one side, or until browned. Cook the other side the same way. Place a bagel half on each plate and spread evenly with the avocado mixture. Divide the seitan/sauekraut mixture evenly among the bagels. Put the tops on and serve.

### SERVING SUGGESTIONS AND VARIATIONS

If you're pressed for time but have some cold cuts on hand, omit the filling and spread. Smear the French toast bagels with mustard and mayo, then layer with the cold cuts. Skip the sauerkraut and you're good to go!

# BERRY-STUFFED FRENCH TOAST POCKETS

Buttery and rich, with a fruity surprise hidden inside, this unconventional French toast will make a popular (and short-lived) appearance on the breakfast table. A great recipe for vegan challah bread can be found on www.vegweb.com.

**YIELD**
4 STUFFED POCKETS

4 slices (1½ inches, or 4 cm thick) slightly stale brioche (page 177) or vegan challah bread

½ cup (70 g) fresh raspberries

1 cup (235 ml) full-fat coconut milk or coconut cream, divided

1 tablespoon (8 g) arrowroot powder

1 tablespoon (15 g) maca powder (optional)

2 tablespoons (25 g) sugar

½ teaspoon pure vanilla extract

Pinch of fine sea salt

Nonstick cooking spray

Maple syrup, agave nectar, or brown rice syrup, for serving

Using a paring knife, cut a deep slit across the top in the middle of each slice of bread. This will create your pocket. Stuff with about 2 tablespoons (31 g) fruit. Close the opening by gently pressing the bread together. Set the filled slices aside.

Combine 2 tablespoons (30 ml) of the coconut milk with the arrowroot powder in a medium, shallow dish and stir to dissolve the powder. Add the remaining 14 tablespoons (205 ml) milk, maca powder, sugar, vanilla, and salt and whisk until smooth.

Dip the pockets into the mixture, one at a time, and soak for a few seconds on each side. Let the extra batter drip back down into the dish.

Heat a panini press fitted with smooth plates on high, or use a large skillet. Lightly coat both sides of the pockets with spray. Cook the pockets on medium-low heat until golden brown, about 4 minutes in all if using a closed panini press, or 4 minutes on each side in a skillet.

Drizzle a little of your favorite sweetener on top. Serve warm.

**SERVING SUGGESTIONS AND VARIATIONS**

Not a fan of raspberries? Not a problem: any sort of berry will fit here, be it blueberries, strawberries, or even blackberries. Just be sure to chop larger berries (like strawberries) so that they fit nicely in the pocket.

# SHH-OCOLATE SPREAD PANINI

Shh . . . your loved ones need not know that beans are hiding in this luscious chocolate spread. We've fooled everyone so far. Why beans, you ask? We love decadent sweets, but we're also always interested in creating foods that pack as big a nutritional punch as possible, without altering flavors.

**YIELD**
4 PANINI
3 CUPS (740 G) SPREAD

**FOR SHH-OCOLATE SPREAD**

1 can (15 ounces, or 425 g) cannellini beans, drained and rinsed

¼ cup plus 2 tablespoons (126 g) agave nectar or other liquid sweetener

¼ cup plus 2 tablespoons (90 ml) nondairy milk

1 teaspoon pure vanilla extract

½ teaspoon pure almond extract (optional)

12 ounces (340 g) semisweet chocolate chips, melted

**FOR PANINI**

8 thick slices slightly stale brioche (page 177) or other bread

Nonstick cooking spray or nondairy butter, if using bread instead of brioche

**TO MAKE THE SPREAD:** Combine the beans, agave, milk, vanilla, and almond extract in a food processor. Process until perfectly smooth. Add the chocolate and process again until perfectly smooth, stopping to scrape the sides with a rubber spatula. Store in an airtight container in the fridge. To use as a spread, let sit at room temperature for 15 minutes. To use as syrup, slowly heat on the stove in a small saucepan over low heat until it reaches a syrupy consistency.

**TO ASSEMBLE THE PANINI:** Spread 3 tablespoons (46 g) of the spread (or enough to cover the surface) on 4 of the slices of brioche. (You will have spread left over; save it for another use.) Top each with another slice. Heat a panini press fitted with smooth plates on high, or heat a large skillet over medium heat. Lightly coat with spray or butter. Cook in batches over medium-low heat, without closing the panini press (if using). Flip the sandwich after 5 minutes, or when golden brown, and cook the other side until golden brown. Serve immediately.

**SERVING SUGGESTIONS AND VARIATIONS**

• To make these sandwiches more travel-friendly, don't prepare them as panini. Instead, spread one side of the (not stale, in this case) brioche or bread with nut butter and the other with Shh-ocolate Spread, add a few slices of banana or strawberries in the middle, and wrap it all up tightly to take this show on the road.

• Replace some of the milk in the spread with more sweetener if you like super-sweet things.

• For an extra boost of flavor, add ⅓ cup (85 g) any creamy and toasted nut butter while processing the spread.

# PISTACHIO SPREAD & STRAWBERRY CANAPÉS

These über cute canapés are the perfect after-school snack for kids of all ages. We recommend strawberries here, because their beautiful redness makes for a great contrast to the green of the pistachio spread, but consider using other fresh or dried fruit, or even, dare we say, chocolate chips.

**YIELD**
ABOUT 12 SMALL CANAPÉS,
1½ CUPS (375 G) SPREAD

**FOR SPREAD**

1½ cups (185 g) dry-roasted, unsalted, shelled pistachios

Pinch of sea salt

3 tablespoons (63 g) agave nectar or (45 ml) pure maple syrup

¾ cup (180 ml) nondairy milk, or as needed

**FOR CANAPÉS**

6 slices whole-grain sandwich bread, crusts removed

12 fresh strawberries, hulled and sliced

**TO MAKE THE SPREAD:** Place the pistachios, salt, and agave in a blender, or use a handheld blender, or even better, a high-speed blender. Begin to blend and pour in just enough milk to obtain a spreadable but not too liquid consistency. You can make it as smooth as you want or leave it a little chunkier. Store in an airtight container in the fridge for up to a week.

**TO ASSEMBLE THE CANAPÉS:** Using 2-inch (5-cm), fun-shaped cookie cutters (hearts, stars, animals), stamp shapes out of the slices of bread. (Waste not, want not: use the remnants of those slices to make bread crumbs!) Apply enough pistachio spread to generously cover the whole surface of the bread. Top each with a sliced strawberry, and serve.

**SERVING SUGGESTIONS AND VARIATIONS**

Turn these canapés into traveling wonders by using the pistachio spread as you would any nut butter. Spread generously on one whole slice of your favorite bread, add some Shh-ocolate Spread (page 26) on another slice, merge the two slices, pack it all tightly, grab a piece of fruit to eat with it, and off you go to face the day!

# MAPLE-NUT PIE WAFFLEWICH

A little autumnal, spicy decadence bright and early is a good thing. If you're like us, you might want to consider doubling the recipe for the walnut filling here, just for kicks—we highly recommend it on top of ice cream or stirred into your morning bowl of oatmeal.

**FOR FILLING**

2 tablespoons (30 ml) water

2 tablespoons (28 g) nondairy butter

⅓ cup (73 g) packed light brown sugar

2 teaspoons ground cinnamon

Pinch of fine sea salt

1 cup (100 g) pecan or (120 g) walnut pieces

½ teaspoon pure vanilla extract

**FOR WAFFLES**

1 cup (235 ml) soymilk

1 tablespoon (15 ml) apple cider vinegar or fresh lemon juice

3 tablespoons (45 ml) canola oil

¼ cup (55 g) packed light brown sugar

2 teaspoons maple extract

½ teaspoon fine sea salt

1½ cups (180 g) whole wheat pastry flour

1 teaspoon baking powder

½ teaspoon baking soda

Nonstick cooking spray

**TO MAKE THE FILLING:** Combine the water, butter, sugar, cinnamon, and salt in a small saucepan. Cook over medium-high heat for about 1 minute, stirring constantly, until the butter is melted. Remove from the heat, add the pecans, and stir for about 1 minute (the mixture will continue cooking from the residual heat). Add the vanilla, stir to combine, and set aside until ready to use. The mixture will thicken a little as it cools.

**TO MAKE THE WAFFLES:** Combine the milk and vinegar in a large bowl: the mixture will curdle and become like buttermilk. Stir in the oil, sugar, maple extract, and salt. Add the flour, baking powder, and baking soda and stir until smooth, being careful not to overmix.

Cook the waffles according to the waffle iron instructions using nonstick cooking spray. You should get 2 Belgian-size waffles, or 4 standard-size waffles. (For extra crispness, toast the waffles in a toaster oven before assembling and eating.)

To serve, break the waffles into quarters. Add 2 tablespoons to ¼ cup (34 to 68 g) of filling on top of one quarter, then top with another quarter. Serve warm.

# PLUM-TILLAS WITH VANILLA DIPPING SAUCE

The slight tartness of the plum is paired with the sweet, almost buttery flavor and super-creaminess of the vanilla dipping sauce here. Plus, getting to dip your food into something saucy always makes it more fun to eat.

**YIELD**
4 TORTILLAS, 1½ CUPS
(355 ML) VANILLA SAUCE

### FOR VANILLA DIPPING SAUCE

1 cup (235 ml) unsweetened plain or vanilla soymilk

¼ cup (50 g) granulated sugar

2 teaspoons pure vanilla extract

⅛ to ¼ teaspoon xanthan gum

¼ cup (60 ml) coconut cream or full-fat coconut milk

### FOR PLUMS

6 firm medium-size plums (1 pound, or 454 g), pitted and cut into bite-size pieces

1 teaspoon nondairy butter, melted

1 tablespoon (14 g) packed light brown sugar

1 teaspoon balsamic vinegar

1 teaspoon water

### FOR TORTILLAS

Four 9-inch (23-cm) flour tortillas

Nonstick cooking spray

**TO MAKE THE SAUCE:** Combine all the ingredients (start with only ⅛ teaspoon xanthan gum, adding more if needed to obtain a yogurtlike texture) together in a blender. Blend until perfectly smooth and somewhat thick, like yogurt. Refrigerate in an airtight container for at least 3 hours before using.

**TO MAKE THE PLUMS:** Place the plums in a skillet and combine with the butter, sugar, vinegar, and water. Sauté over medium heat until all the liquid evaporates and the plums are just tender but not mushy, about 4 minutes. Remove from the heat and set aside.

**TO ASSEMBLE THE TORTILLAS:** Preheat a panini press fitted with smooth or grill plates on high heat. Place the equivalent of one and a half plums evenly on half of each tortilla and fold over the other half. Lightly coat both sides of the tortilla with spray, close the panini press, and cook until golden brown and crispy, about 6 minutes in all. Cut each tortilla into 4 triangles and dip into the vanilla sauce as desired.

### SERVING SUGGESTIONS AND VARIATIONS

• No panini press? Preheat the oven to 400°F (200°C, or gas mark 6). Lightly coat a baking sheet with nonstick spray. Place the folded tortillas on the sheet and lightly spray the tops with nonstick spray. Bake for 5 to 7 minutes, until crisp. Cut and serve.

• Alternatively, use a grill pan with a press, following the same instructions as when using a panini press.

# APRICOT BREAKFAST PANINI

What is better than cinnamon bread? Not much. But this slightly tart apricot jam sandwich is a new (and delicious!) way to enjoy it. Keep it in mind for days when you just can't face another piece of cinnamon toast. And let us know when that happens, because you'd be the first!

**YIELD**
4 SANDWICHES
1½ CUPS (300 G) JAM

### FOR QUICK APRICOT JAM

12 ounces (340 g) fresh apricots, halved, pitted, and chopped

2 tablespoons (15 g) dried sweetened tart cherries

¼ cup plus 2 tablespoons (90 ml) fresh orange juice, divided

1 to 2 tablespoons (21 to 42 g) agave nectar

Pinch of grated nutmeg

2 tablespoons (16 g) cornstarch

### FOR SANDWICHES

8 slices (½-inch, or 1.3-cm thick) Cinnamon Swirl Bread (page 176)

2 tablespoons (28 g) nondairy butter

¼ cup (60 g) nondairy cream cheese

**TO MAKE THE JAM:** In a small saucepan over medium heat, combine the apricots, cherries, ¼ cup (60 ml) of the orange juice, 1 tablespoon (21 g) of the agave, and nutmeg. Bring the mixture to a boil, then reduce the heat to a simmer and allow the apricots to break down some, 4 to 5 minutes. It should be chunky, but not have large pieces of fruit. In a small bowl, combine the remaining 2 tablespoons (30 ml) orange juice and the cornstarch. Add to the mixture and stir until thickened, 3 to 4 minutes. Taste and add the remaining 1 tablespoon (21 g) agave if needed. The jam thickens as it cools, so make it ahead of time and refrigerate in an airtight container until you're ready to use it.

**TO ASSEMBLE THE SANDWICHES:** Preheat a panini press. Butter one side of each slice of bread. On the unbuttered sides, spread 1 tablespoon (15 g) of the cream cheese and 2 tablespoons (40 g) of the jam (you will have extra jam left over; save it for another use). Try to keep the jam away from the edges of the bread so it will not seep out. Put the top slice of bread on so that both the buttered sides are facing out. Close the panini press and cook for 5 to 7 minutes, or until golden brown.

> **SERVING SUGGESTIONS AND VARIATIONS**
> - Cut into quarters, these are a terrific addition to a breakfast or brunch spread.
> - If you're short on time, feel free to substitute any jam you have on hand. We prefer the naturally sweetened variety.

# BLUEBERRY AND CORN PANCAKE SANDWICHES WITH LEMONY FILLING

These mini pancakes capture summer. There's no need to cook the corn on the cob, but if yours is precooked, that's fine, too. Bursting with blueberries and a tangy lemon cream, these sandwiches will make you feel like you're having dessert for breakfast.

**YIELD**
6 SANDWICHES

### FOR FILLING

¼ cup plus 2 tablespoons (51 g) cashews, soaked in water for 1 hour, then drained

¼ cup plus 2 tablespoons (89 ml) fresh lemon juice

1 tablespoon (6 g) lemon zest

1 tablespoon plus 2 teaspoons (25 g) nondairy cream cheese

1 tablespoon plus 1 teaspoon (28 g) agave nectar

Pinch of fine sea salt

### FOR PANCAKES

1 cup plus 2 tablespoons (265 ml) soymilk

2 tablespoons (30 ml) fresh lemon juice

2 tablespoons (25 g) sugar

1 tablespoon (15 ml) canola oil

½ teaspoon fine sea salt

½ teaspoon dried thyme

½ teaspoon lemon zest

1 cup (125 g) all-purpose flour

¼ cup (32 g) finely ground cornmeal

1 tablespoon (12 g) baking powder

1¼ cups (183 g) fresh blueberries, divided

½ cup (77 g) fresh or frozen corn, rinsed

Canola oil, for cooking

Confectioners' sugar, for serving

**TO MAKE THE FILLING:** In a blender, blend all the ingredients until completely smooth. Refrigerate in an airtight container until ready to use.

**TO MAKE THE PANCAKES:** In a medium-size bowl, combine the milk and lemon juice; the mixture will curdle and become like buttermilk. Stir in the sugar, canola oil, salt, thyme, and lemon zest. Add the flour, cornmeal, and baking powder. Stir to combine; a few lumps are okay. Stir in ¾ cup (110 g) blueberries and the corn.

Preheat the oven to 300°F (150°C, or gas mark 2). Lightly coat a large skillet with oil and place over medium heat. Working in batches, scoop ¼ cup (57 g) of batter into the skillet for each pancake. Cook for 3 to 4 minutes, or until the edges look set and bubbles are appearing on the tops of the pancakes. The bottoms should be golden brown. Flip and cook the other side for 2 to 3 minutes. Keep warm in the oven until all the pancakes are cooked. You should get 12 pancakes.

**TO ASSEMBLE THE SANDWICHES,** place 6 pancakes on plates. Top with a generous tablespoon (14 g) of filling and a generous tablespoon (9 g) of the remaining blueberries. Top with the remaining 6 pancakes. Dust with confectioners' sugar and serve.

### SERVING SUGGESTIONS AND VARIATIONS

If you're not keen on blueberries, try this with strawberries or blackberries instead.

# CHAPTER THREE

## GOING TOPLESS

{ **BREAD ON THE BOTTOM, FILLING ON TOP: RATED R FOR RAVENOUS** }

These sandwiches bring a strong foundation to the plate. Literally. Stacked and spread with all kinds of wonderfulness, you'll need lots of napkins (and sometimes a fork and knife) for these sandwiches. Think of them as being so incredible that they just can't be restrained by that top slice of bread. Nothing can keep these "fillings" down!

◄ *Onion Ring Ranchocado,*
page 38

# ONION RING RANCHOCADO

Ranch dressing, meet avocado. Avocado, meet ranch dressing. Beer-battered onion rings are joining the party, too. You're all going to get along famously. For this one use the bigger, outer rings of the onion. Save the inner rings for scrambles *(pictured on page 36)*.

*(pictured on page 36)*

**YIELD**
4 SANDWICHES

## FOR SPREAD

1 large avocado, pitted, peeled, and cut into chunks

¼ cup (56 g) vegan mayonnaise

1 tablespoon (15 ml) apple cider vinegar

1 tablespoon (10 g) chopped shallot

1 tablespoon (4 g) minced fresh parsley

2 teaspoons minced fresh thyme

2 teaspoons minced fresh dill

Salt and pepper, to taste

## FOR ONION RINGS

1 cup (235 ml) vegan beer, chilled

2 teaspoons sriracha

1 teaspoon liquid smoke

1 teaspoon yellow mustard

½ teaspoon fine sea salt

Pinch of black pepper

1 cup (125 g) all-purpose flour, plus more if needed

Canola oil, for cooking

12 large (¾ inch, or 2 cm wide) sweet onion rings, separated

## FOR SANDWICHES

2 crusty ciabatta rolls, cut in half and toasted

2 cups (144 g) shredded lettuce

8 slices tomato

Sriracha, for serving

**TO MAKE THE SPREAD:** In a blender, combine the avocado, mayonnaise, vinegar, and shallot. Blend until smooth. Stir in the herbs. Season to taste with salt and pepper.

**TO MAKE THE ONION RINGS:** Preheat the oven to 300°F (150°C, or gas mark 2). In a medium-size bowl, whisk together the beer, sriracha, liquid smoke, mustard, salt, and pepper. Add the flour and whisk until smooth. The mixture should coat the onion ring well without dripping off. Add 1 tablespoon (8 g) flour or (15 ml) beer if needed. Line a baking sheet with paper towels. Heat 1 inch (2.5 cm) canola oil in a heavy-bottomed pan over medium-high heat. Working in batches, dip the onion rings into the mixture, then slide into the hot oil. The oil should sizzle but not ripple. Adjust the heat if necessary. Be careful not to crowd the pan or the oil temperature will drop. Cook the onion rings for 1 to 2 minutes, or until golden brown. Drain on the baking sheet. Keep warm in the oven until all are cooked. Repeat with the remaining onion rings.

**TO ASSEMBLE THE SANDWICHES:** Spread the sauce on the inside of the rolls. Layer on the lettuce, then the tomatoes. Top with the onion rings. Pass the extra sriracha at the table.

### SERVING SUGGESTIONS AND VARIATIONS

- For a more substantial meal, add one of our burgers to this sandwich (pages 108 to 110).
- Don't hesitate to enjoy these onion rings alongside any sandwich.

# CRISPY LEEK-MUSHROOM MANIA SANDWICHES

Herb-dressed mushrooms make these sandwiches hearty, while the intensely flavored spread makes them irresistible. Testers liked this versatile spread so much that they doubled it to keep some on hand for other sandwiches. Our testers are always right, by the way.

**YIELD**
4 SANDWICHES

**FOR SPREAD**

¼ cup (56 g) vegan mayonnaise

2 tablespoons (4 g) chopped moist sun-dried tomatoes

1 tablespoon (10 g) chopped red onion

1 tablespoon (15 ml) fresh lemon juice

**FOR MUSHROOMS**

1 tablespoon (15 ml) olive oil

4 large portobello mushrooms, stems removed, sliced

1 pound (454 g) mushrooms of choice, sliced

¼ teaspoon dried thyme

¼ teaspoon lemon pepper

¼ teaspoon black pepper

1 clove garlic, minced

2 tablespoons (30 ml) fresh lemon juice

1 tablespoon (15 ml) tamari

Salt, to taste

**FOR CRISPY LEEKS**

2 leeks, white part only, washed, patted dry, and sliced into ¼-inch (6-mm) rounds for a total of 1 cup (140 g)

1 tablespoon (8 g) all-purpose flour

¼ teaspoon lemon pepper

¼ teaspoon fine sea salt

Canola oil, for cooking

**FOR SANDWICHES**

4 slices bread, toasted

**TO MAKE THE SPREAD:** Combine all the ingredients in a blender. Blend until smooth. Refrigerate in an airtight container until ready to use.

**TO MAKE THE MUSHROOMS:** Heat the oil in a large skillet over medium heat. Add the mushrooms. Cook, stirring occasionally, for 10 minutes, or until the mushrooms are softened and have released their juices. Add the thyme, lemon pepper, black pepper, garlic, lemon juice, and tamari. Increase the heat to high and cook for 4 minutes, or until most of the liquid has either been absorbed or cooked off. Season with salt to taste.

**TO MAKE THE LEEKS:** In a medium-size bowl, combine the leeks, flour, lemon pepper, and salt. Toss to coat. Line a plate with paper towels. In a large skillet, heat about ¼ inch (6 mm) canola oil over medium heat. Cooking in batches, add half the leeks. Cook, stirring occasionally, for 3 to 4 minutes, or until golden. Do not burn. Remove from the skillet with a slotted spoon and drain on the paper towels. Repeat with the second batch.

**TO ASSEMBLE THE SANDWICHES:** Spread the mayonnaise blend on one side of each piece of toast. Top with the mushrooms and the leeks, and serve.

---

**SERVING SUGGESTIONS AND VARIATIONS**

If you're lucky enough to have leftover crispy leeks, try them as "croutons" on a salad or as a garnish for a bowl of soup.

# BEANS NOT ON TOAST

Before someone hits us over the head for not being authentic here, let us just say we've never had beans on toast, but we fear soggy bread. Which isn't to say that authentic recipes yield soggy bread, but we like how these waffles won't get floppy on you while you enjoy your beans.

**YIELD**
4 OR 8 SANDWICHES

### FOR BREAD WAFFLES

2 tablespoons (30 ml) sesame oil

1 tablespoon (21 g) agave nectar

1 cup (235 ml) plain nondairy milk, lukewarm

2 tablespoons (30 ml) fresh lemon juice

1 teaspoon fine sea salt

Scant 3 cups (360 g) all-purpose flour

2 teaspoons instant yeast

Nonstick cooking spray

### FOR BEANS

1 tablespoon (15 ml) olive oil

4 large tomatoes, diced small

1/3 cup (50 g) minced shallot

6 cloves garlic, minced

1/4 cup (60 ml) apple cider vinegar

1/4 cup (66 g) tomato paste

2 teaspoons vegan Worcestershire sauce

2 cans (15 ounces, or 425 g each) pinto beans, drained and rinsed

1/2 teaspoon smoked sea salt, to taste

1/4 teaspoon coarse black pepper, to taste

### FOR SANDWICHES

Nondairy butter, for serving

Chopped fresh parsley, for serving

**TO MAKE THE WAFFLES:** Combine the oil, agave, milk, juice, and salt in a large bowl. Add the flour and yeast and stir for a few minutes, stabbing the dough with a spatula to make sure it gets kneaded. Cover and let rise for 2 hours, until its size doubles.

Punch down the dough and divide it into 4 or 8 equal portions; the dough will be sticky, so moisten your hands if needed. Use a heaping 1/2 cup (155 g) dough for 4 portions or 1/4 cup (78 g) for 8 portions. Place portions on a piece of parchment paper and let rest for 15 minutes.

Following the manufacturer's instructions, heat a waffle iron and coat lightly with spray. Place one (if using a standard waffle iron) or two (if using a large and wide Belgian waffle iron) portions of dough on the iron and press closed for a few seconds to spread the dough. Bake for 8 minutes, or until golden brown and the edges of the waffles aren't doughy. Cool waffles on a wire rack. Repeat with the remaining dough.

**TO MAKE THE BEANS:** Heat the oil in a large skillet. Add the tomatoes, shallot, and garlic. Cook over medium-high heat for 2 minutes, until the tomatoes get saucy. Combine the vinegar, tomato paste, and Worcestershire sauce in a small bowl. Add to the pan, and cook for 1 minute. Add the beans, salt, and pepper, and cook for 2 minutes longer, stirring occasionally.

**TO ASSEMBLE THE SANDWICHES:** Spread butter on each waffle. Divide the bean mixture among the waffles, sprinkle with a little parsley, and serve.

# 'SHROOMS ON A SHINGLE

During World War II, a version of this sandwich was a mainstay for American soldiers. There are many variations, but we opted for brown gravy rather than white and added some vibrant Italian flavors. The portobellos make this a hearty and filling meal.

**YIELD**
4 SANDWICHES

**FOR TOPPING**

2 teaspoons olive oil

2 teaspoons nondairy butter

¼ cup (40 g) minced shallot

4 large portobello mushrooms, stemmed, gilled, and cut into ½-inch (1.3-cm) slices

1 pound (454 g) other mushrooms of choice, cut into ¼-inch (6-mm) slices

Salt and pepper, to taste

½ cup (90 g) chopped roasted red bell peppers

2 cloves garlic, minced

1 tablespoon (9 g) drained capers

Pinch of red pepper flakes

¼ cup (10 g) minced fresh basil

1 tablespoon (3 g) minced fresh chives

2 tablespoons (30 ml) fresh lemon juice

1¼ cups (295 ml) vegetable broth, divided

1 tablespoon (8 g) cornstarch

**FOR GARLIC SHINGLES**

1 tablespoon (14 g) nondairy butter, softened

1 tablespoon (15 ml) olive oil

2 cloves garlic, minced

¼ teaspoon dried thyme

¼ teaspoon dried oregano

¼ teaspoon fine sea salt

Pinch of black pepper

8 slices ciabatta or other Italian-style bread

Minced fresh parsley, for garnish

**TO MAKE THE TOPPING:** Heat the oil and butter in a large skillet over medium heat. Add the shallot, mushrooms, and a pinch of salt and pepper. Cook, stirring occasionally, for 5 minutes, or until the mushrooms start to soften. Add the bell peppers, garlic, capers, pepper flakes, basil, chives, and lemon juice. Stir and cook for 2 minutes. Add 1 cup (235 ml) of the broth to the mixture. In a small bowl, combine the remaining ¼ cup (60 ml) broth with the cornstarch. Whisk until smooth. Add to the mixture and whisk for 3 to 4 minutes, or until thickened. Taste and adjust the seasonings.

**TO MAKE THE SHINGLES:** Set the oven to broil. Combine the butter, oil, garlic, thyme, oregano, salt, and pepper in a small bowl. Mix well. Spread on one side of each slice of bread. Place the bread butter side up on a baking sheet and broil for 2 to 3 minutes, or until golden.

**TO ASSEMBLE THE SANDWICHES:** Place 2 slices of toast on each plate. Spoon ½ cup (124 g) of the topping onto each piece, garnish with the parsley, and serve.

**SERVING SUGGESTIONS AND VARIATIONS**

We've been known to top cooked pasta with the mushroom mixture for a quick comfort food classic.

# SCRAMBLED TOFU & GREENS BRIOCHE'WICH

Celine's mom used to serve eggs on top of wilted spinach and toasted bread every Friday, rain or shine. Here's our veganized take on what used to be (and is again) a favorite meal.

### FOR GREENS

1 tablespoon (15 ml) olive oil

¼ cup (40 g) minced shallot

4 cloves garlic, minced

2 medium-size tomatoes, chopped

Smoked or regular sea salt, to taste

Ground black pepper, to taste

1 pound (454 g) mixed leafy greens (collard, mustard, kale)

¼ cup (60 ml) water

### FOR TOFU

¾ cup (180 ml) unsweetened coconut milk

2 tablespoons (15 g) nutritional yeast

1 tablespoon (15 g) maca powder (optional)

1 tablespoon (8 g) chickpea flour

¼ teaspoon grated nutmeg

¼ teaspoon turmeric

2 cloves garlic, pressed

½ teaspoon smoked or regular sea salt, to taste

Pinch of black salt (optional)

¼ teaspoon ground black pepper, to taste

Nonstick cooking spray

1 pound (454 g) super- or extra-firm tofu, drained, pressed, and cut into ½-inch (1.3-cm) cubes

### FOR SANDWICHES

1 loaf brioche (page 177) halved lengthwise, cut widthwise into 3 even pieces, lightly toasted

Chopped fresh parsley, for serving

1 lemon, cut into 6 wedges

**TO MAKE THE GREENS:** Use a pot large enough to accommodate the amount of greens. Heat the oil in the pot over medium-high heat; add the shallot, garlic, tomatoes, salt, and pepper; and cook for 2 minutes. Stir in the greens. Once the greens start to wilt, add the water and cook, uncovered, for 10 to 15 minutes, until the ribs are tender and the liquid has reduced. Set aside.

**TO MAKE THE TOFU:** Combine the coconut milk, nutritional yeast, maca powder, chickpea flour, nutmeg, turmeric, garlic, salt, and pepper in a medium-size bowl. Heat a large skillet over medium heat. Move it away from the stove once it's warm, and carefully coat it with spray. Add the tofu cubes and cook until golden brown, stirring occasionally, 5 to 7 minutes. Add the sauce, increase the heat to medium-high, and cook for 2 minutes, or until thickened.

**TO ASSEMBLE THE SANDWICHES:** Place ²/₃ cup (122 g) greens on each slice of brioche. Top with ²/₃ cup (100 g) tofu, sprinkle with the parsley, squeeze a few drops of lemon juice on top, and serve.

### SERVING SUGGESTIONS AND VARIATIONS

If you've had a long day and don't have it in you to make brioche, just use 6 large, thick slices of lightly toasted crusty bread in its place.

# HOLLANDAZE'D ASPARAGUS ROUNDS

Hollandaise sauce is one of the five "mother" sauces in French cooking. That means it is the base that is used in other sauces. Although unorthodox, this unique version is a handy one to have under your vegan belt. It's adaptable and can take you places.

**YIELD**
4 SANDWICHES

### FOR HOLLANDAZE SAUCE

½ cup (69 g) cashews, soaked in water for 1 hour, then rinsed and drained

⅓ cup plus 1 tablespoon (95 ml) nondairy milk

¼ cup (60 g) sauerkraut, drained but not squeezed dry

2 tablespoons (30 ml) fresh lemon juice

1 tablespoon plus 1 teaspoon (20 ml) apple cider vinegar

1 tablespoon (15 ml) olive oil

1 teaspoon Dijon mustard

1 teaspoon nutritional yeast

¼ teaspoon fine sea salt, to taste

¼ teaspoon sriracha, to taste

Pinch of white pepper

### FOR ASPARAGUS

12 ounces (340 g) asparagus, cut into 4-inch (10-cm) pieces

1 tablespoon (15 ml) olive oil

Salt and pepper, to taste

### FOR SANDWICHES

1 large tomato, cut into four ½-inch (1.3-cm) slices

2 English muffins, split and toasted

Minced fresh chives, for serving

**TO MAKE THE SAUCE:** Combine all the ingredients in a blender and blend until smooth. Taste and adjust the seasonings. Just before serving, heat over medium heat in a small saucepan, stirring often. Add an extra tablespoon (15 ml) milk if needed for a pourable consistency.

**TO MAKE THE ASPARAGUS:** Preheat the oven to 400°F (200°C, or gas mark 6). In a 9 x 13-inch (23 x 33-cm) pan, toss the asparagus with olive oil, salt, and pepper. Roast in the oven for 10 minutes, or until tender.

**TO ASSEMBLE THE SANDWICHES:** Place the tomato slices on the muffin halves. Divide the asparagus evenly on top of the tomato slices. Pour a generous ¼ cup (60 ml) sauce over each half, sprinkle with the chives, serve.

---

**SERVING SUGGESTIONS AND VARIATIONS**

• Feeling extra hungry? Add broiled or pan-fried tofu to the sandwich.

• Although we suggest asparagus here, feel free to sub steamed or roasted broccoli, or sautéed greens. The sauce brightens up any vegetable.

# NAVAJO TACOS

Indian tacos are made with fried bread and topped with the typical items found on Latin-style tacos. You can go all out and add nondairy sour cream and cheese on top, or keep it simple if you prefer.

**YIELD**
4 TACOS

## FOR CHICKPEA CHORIZO

1 can (15 ounces, or 425 g) chickpeas, drained and rinsed

1 tablespoon (15 ml) olive oil

¼ to ½ teaspoon cayenne pepper, to taste

1 teaspoon paprika

Smoked sea salt, to taste

1 tablespoon (15 ml) apple cider vinegar

1 tablespoon (15 ml) fresh lime juice

1 teaspoon ground cumin

2 tablespoons (30 g) ketchup

1 teaspoon onion powder

1 clove garlic, minced

## FOR BREAD

1 cup (125 g) all-purpose flour, plus ½ cup (63 g) for rolling

1 teaspoon onion powder

1 teaspoon dried cilantro

½ teaspoon fine sea salt

Ground black pepper, to taste

1 teaspoon baking powder

½ cup (120 ml) water

Vegetable or peanut oil, for frying

## FOR TACOS

1⅓ cups (95 g) shredded lettuce

Heaping ½ cup (160 g) corn salsa

Heaping ½ cup (160 g) tomato salsa

1 avocado, pitted, peeled, and sliced (optional)

Chopped fresh parsley or cilantro, for garnish

1 fresh lime, cut into wedges

**TO MAKE THE CHICKPEA CHORIZO:** Combine all the ingredients in a large skillet. Cook over medium-high heat for about 4 minutes, stirring occasionally, until the liquid has been absorbed. Set aside.

**TO MAKE THE BREAD:** Combine 1 cup (125 g) of flour, onion powder, cilantro, salt, pepper, and baking powder in a large bowl. Add the water, and mix thoroughly. Let stand for 15 minutes at room temperature. Divide the sticky dough into 4 equal portions. On a floured surface, with about ½ cup (63 g) extra flour handy and your hands sufficiently floured, flatten each portion of dough (sprinkling it with flour, but not kneading the flour in) into a 6-inch (15-cm) disk.

Fill a deep 10-inch (25-cm) pot with 1 inch (2.5 cm) of oil. Preheat to 350°F (180°C) on a deep-frying thermometer. Carefully add one disk of dough at a time to the hot oil and cook for 3 minutes on each side, or until golden brown. Transfer to a plate lined with paper towels to absorb excess oil. Repeat with the remaining 3 disks, bringing the oil back up to temperature between batches.

**TO ASSEMBLE THE TACOS:** Top the fried bread with ⅓ cup (24 g) lettuce, 2 heaping tablespoons (40 g) corn salsa, 2 heaping tablespoons (40 g) tomato salsa, a generous ⅓ cup (106 g) chickpea chorizo, and one-fourth of the avocado slices. Garnish with the parsley or cilantro and serve with the lime wedges.

# WELSH RAREBIT

Cheesy vegan goodness baked on top of bread is what this treat is all about! The original, nonvegan recipe comes to us from Wales, as the name indicates. We're especially proud of this one because it got the expert approval of the British nonvegan husband of super-tester Liz Wyman. Serve with caramelized onions, dried or fresh figs, a dollop of vegan brown steak sauce, or sandwich pickles.

**YIELD**
4 SANDWICHES
2 CUPS (480 G) SAUCE

## FOR SAUCE

1 cup (235 ml) unsweetened plain soymilk

½ cup (120 ml) vegan lager beer

¼ cup (56 g) nondairy butter

½ teaspoon paprika

½ teaspoon fine sea salt, to taste

2 cloves garlic

1 teaspoon onion powder

2 teaspoons Dijon mustard

1 tablespoon (16 g) tahini

1 tablespoon (15 g) maca powder (optional)

3 tablespoons (23 g) nutritional yeast

1 teaspoon vegan Worcestershire sauce

¼ cup (20 g) quick-cooking oats

2 teaspoons cornstarch

## FOR SANDWICHES

4 slightly stale crusty bread rolls about 4 inches (10 cm) wide, cut in half, or 8 thick slices any slightly stale crusty bread

**TO MAKE THE SAUCE:** Combine all the ingredients in a blender. Blend until smooth. Place in a microwave-safe bowl and heat for 4 minutes, until thickened. Alternatively, cook in a saucepan over medium-high heat until thickened, about 4 minutes, whisking constantly. Remove from the heat.

**TO ASSEMBLE THE SANDWICHES:** Preheat the oven to 375°F (190°C, or gas mark 5). Line a baking sheet with parchment paper or a silicone baking mat. Spread no more than ¼ cup (60 g) sauce on top of each roll half. Bake for 20 minutes, or until the sauce is set and golden brown on top.

Let cool for about 10 minutes before eating so as not to burn your palate or hands because the sauce and bread will be hot, hot, hot.

Any leftover sauce will keep, in an airtight container in the fridge, for up to 4 days.

### SERVING SUGGESTIONS AND VARIATIONS

There won't be leftovers of the sauce if you make the full recipe of Welsh Rarebits as written, but we must say the sauce is quite stellar when used on baked potatoes, if you want to take a break from bread. Bake whole, large unpeeled potatoes until just tender, hollow them out, mash and mix the flesh with some of the rarebit sauce, place the mixture back into the potato shells, and bake again until golden brown on top.

# PUFF PASTRY POT PIE SANDWICHES

Pot pies are comfort food favorites. We dressed them up a little with the addition of Marsala wine. Puff pastry has a way of classing up a place. It does that and more in this dish.

2 tablespoons (30 ml) canola oil, divided

2 No Cluck Cutlets (page 181), diced

⅓ cup (50 g) minced shallot

1 cup (110 g) diced yellow potato

⅔ cup (87 g) peeled and diced carrots

2 tablespoons (15 g) minced celery

1 cup (112 g) sliced cremini mushrooms

1 clove garlic, minced

½ teaspoon dried thyme

¼ teaspoon dried rosemary

⅛ teaspoon cayenne pepper

1 tablespoon (8 g) all-purpose flour

2 tablespoons (30 ml) Marsala wine

1 cup (235 ml) vegetable broth, plus more if needed

¼ cup (32 g) fresh or thawed frozen peas

1 tablespoon (4 g) minced fresh parsley

Salt and pepper, to taste

½ sheet puff pastry (4 x 9 inches, or 10 x 23 cm), thawed

Heat 1 tablespoon (15 ml) of the canola oil in a large skillet over medium heat. Add the diced cutlets, shallot, potato, carrot, and celery. Cook for 6 minutes, stirring often, until the diced cutlets are lightly browned.

Add the remaining 1 tablespoon (15 ml) canola oil, the mushrooms, garlic, thyme, rosemary, cayenne, and flour. Cook, stirring occasionally, for 4 minutes. Add the wine to deglaze the skillet, stirring to incorporate anything that may be stuck to the bottom. Add the broth, bring to a boil, then reduce to a simmer. Partially cover and cook for 20 minutes, or until the potatoes are tender, stirring occasionally. Add more broth if needed. Stir in the peas and parsley. Season to taste with salt and pepper.

Meanwhile, cut the puff pastry in half to form 2 pieces 4 x 4½ inches (10 x 11 cm). Bake as per the package directions. When cool enough to handle, gently split the puffed squares in half to make 4 pieces. Divide the pot pie filling evenly over the puff pastry and serve.

**SERVING SUGGESTIONS AND VARIATIONS**

- If you can't find vegan puff pastry, serve this on toast slices.
- The topping is also fantastic on baked potatoes. Just omit the potatoes from the mixture, and then slice and stuff the baked potato.

# PESTO PITZAS

If you make the cheese ahead of time, you can serve this as a ready-in-no-time appetizer or snack, or even as a meal alongside a huge plate of mixed greens, thinly sliced tomatoes, and slivers of onion with a light homemade dressing.

**YIELD**
4 PITZAS
1 POUND (454 G) CHEESE

## FOR CHEESE

Nonstick cooking spray

1 cup (235 ml) unsweetened coconut cream (see page 13)

½ cup (120 g) drained firm silken tofu

1 or 2 cloves garlic, to taste

¾ teaspoon smoked sea salt

½ to 1 teaspoon liquid smoke, to taste

½ teaspoon ground white pepper, to taste

½ teaspoon onion powder

1 tablespoon (15 ml) fresh lemon juice

1 to 2 tablespoons (8 to 15 g) nutritional yeast, to taste

1 tablespoon (16 g) almond or cashew butter

1 tablespoon (8 g) agar powder

## FOR PESTO

1½ cups (36 g) fresh basil leaves

1 or 2 cloves garlic, to taste, pressed

Salt and ground black pepper, to taste

1½ tablespoons (25 ml) fresh lemon juice

¼ to ½ cup (60 to 120 ml) extra-virgin olive oil, as needed

## FOR PITZAS

Four 8-inch (20-cm) pita breads

2 tablespoons (16 g) drained capers

¼ cup (28 g) chopped oil-packed sun-dried tomatoes

**TO MAKE THE CHEESE:** Lightly coat a 2½-inch (6.4-cm)-deep 16-ounce (454-g) round dish with spray. Combine all the ingredients in a blender and process until smooth. Transfer to a medium-size saucepan and cook over medium-high heat for 5 minutes, whisking constantly. The mixture will thicken slightly and become more cohesive; it will thicken more as it cools. Pour into the prepared dish, cover, and chill overnight in the fridge. It will keep for up to 1 week, stored in an airtight container. To use, finely grate 1 cup (75 g) for the sandwiches and save the rest for another use.

**TO MAKE THE PESTO:** Place the basil and garlic in a food processor. Pulse a few times to chop the basil. Add salt and pepper to taste, then add the lemon juice. Slowly drizzle in the oil through the hole in the lid while the machine is running, until a paste forms.

**TO ASSEMBLE THE PITZAS:** Preheat the oven to 375°F (190°C, or gas mark 5). Spread pesto on each pita bread to cover the surface. Sprinkle ¼ cup (19 g) cheese on top, then add ½ tablespoon (4 g) capers and 1 tablespoon (7 g) sun-dried tomatoes. Bake for 15 minutes, or until golden brown and crispy.

### RECIPE NOTES

• You'll have an easier time grating the cheese if you wrap it well and freeze it for a few hours, so it becomes firmer.

• These pitzas taste great eaten cold too, kind of like crackers, and can therefore be taken on the road if you let them cool completely before wrapping them tightly.

# HOT BROWN SANDWICHES

The Hot Brown has been a Kentucky favorite since its debut at the Brown Hotel in Louisville in 1926. Originally made with turkey, bacon, and cheese sauce, this sandwich has been veganized and healthified with slightly smoky tofu bits, creamy garlic sauce, and a green vegetable to boot!

**YIELD**
4 SANDWICHES

### FOR SAUCE

12 cloves garlic, toasted (see Note)

⅓ cup plus 1 tablespoon (48 g) nutritional yeast

1 teaspoon onion powder

1 teaspoon mustard powder

½ teaspoon turmeric

1 cup (235 ml) coconut milk

2 teaspoons white miso

½ cup (120 ml) vegetable broth, chilled

2 tablespoons (16 g) cornstarch

### FOR BROCCOLINI

12 ounces (340 g) broccolini

⅓ cup (80 ml) vegetable broth

Pinch of fine sea salt

Pinch of black pepper

### FOR SANDWICHES

Four 1-inch (2.5-cm) slices sandwich bread, toasted

1 large tomato, cut into ½-inch (1.3-cm) slices

1 recipe Tofu Bits (page 67)

**TO MAKE THE SAUCE:** In a blender, combine the garlic, nutritional yeast, onion powder, mustard powder, turmeric, coconut milk, and miso. Blend until smooth. Transfer to a small saucepan and cook over medium heat. Whisk the broth and cornstarch together in a small bowl. Whisk into the sauce and continue to whisk until thickened, 3 to 5 minutes.

**TO MAKE THE BROCCOLINI:** In a large skillet over high heat, combine the broccolini, broth, salt, and pepper and cook for 6 to 7 minutes, or until tender and the broth has evaporated.

**TO ASSEMBLE THE SANDWICHES:** Preheat the oven to 400°F (200°C, or gas mark 6). Place the toast slices on a large baking sheet. Divide the tomato slices and broccolini among the bread. Top evenly with the sauce and tofu. Bake for 5 minutes, or until the sauce begins to bubble. Serve.

### RECIPE NOTE

To toast garlic, peel the garlic cloves and place in a small cast-iron skillet over medium-high heat. Stir and toast for 4 to 5 minutes, or until golden

### SERVING SUGGESTIONS AND VARIATIONS

The sauce doesn't taste too strongly of coconut, but if you are a coconut hater, you could replace half or all of it with unsweetened soy or almond creamer.

# CABANA CHEESE SANDWICHES

Even though it's been a decade since we last partook, this sandwich is pretty close to how we remember cottage cheese to be. We focused on a savory version because sweet cottage cheese served with pineapple never really was our cup of tea, but you could remove the pepper, herbs, onion, and garlic and add just a little sweetener for a pineapple version, if you fancy.

| YIELD |
|---|
| 4 SANDWICHES |

**FOR CABANA CHEESE**

15 ounces (425 g) extra-firm tofu, crumbled small but not mashed

½ cup (120 g) unsweetened plain nondairy yogurt

3 tablespoons (45 ml) light olive oil

1 to 2 tablespoons (15 to 30 ml) apple cider vinegar, to taste

½ teaspoon ground black pepper, to taste

½ teaspoon fine sea salt

½ teaspoon dried dillweed or 2 teaspoons chopped fresh chives

2 tablespoons (20 g) chopped shallot or red onion

1 clove garlic, pressed

**FOR SANDWICHES**

4 large Boston, Bibb, or butter lettuce leaves

4 thick slices Green Monster Bread (page 178) or any crusty bread, lightly toasted

¾ cup (104 g) chopped tomato

4 slices sandwich pickles (optional)

**TO MAKE THE CABANA CHEESE:** Place the tofu in a fine-mesh sieve lined with cheesecloth, set over a bowl, and drain for several hours in the fridge. Combine the remaining ingredients in a large bowl. Add the drained tofu and stir to combine, being careful not to crush the tofu. Chill again for a few hours in an airtight container, to let the flavors meld.

**TO ASSEMBLE THE SANDWICHES:** Lay 1 lettuce leaf on a slice of bread. Gently stir the chopped tomato into the cabana cheese. When moving the cabana cheese from its main bowl, use a slotted spoon to avoid the extra liquid that could make the sandwiches soggy. Top the lettuce with ⅓ cup (80 g) cabana cheese and a pickle, and serve immediately. If you don't plan on eating the sandwiches immediately, prepare them right before serving to prevent sogginess.

**SERVING SUGGESTIONS AND VARIATIONS**

Make this one close-faced if you want to take it on the road, but be sure to choose a crustier bread and protect it from any unwanted moisture by draining the cabana cheese thoroughly and covering every inch of the bread with the most wilt-resistant lettuce you can find. Pack it tightly, put it in your cooler, and watch it magically become travel-friendly.

# CHAPTER FOUR

---

# KEEP IT COOL

{ **CHILLED, MAKE-AHEAD
SANDWICHES READY FOR EATING
WHENEVER HUNGER STRIKES** }

These sandwich wonders require minimal cooking. Want another slice of great news? We've got you covered: they also taste as if you put a lot more effort into them than you actually did, which makes them ideal for make-and-take feasting, especially during those sweltering summer months when the last thing you want to do is get anywhere near the stove. You know what this all means, right? More time for fun!

◀ *North End Grinder*, page 56

# NORTH END GRINDER

If you've ever been to the Italian section of Boston, you'll recognize this one *(pictured on page 54)* as soon as you taste the dried herb dressing. Try to use two or more varieties of cold cuts for the best taste. You know as well as we do that homemade cold cuts are ideal here. However, store-bought will do in a pinch.

**YIELD**
4 SANDWICHES
⅔ CUP (160 ML) DRESSING

**FOR DRESSING**

1 teaspoon dried basil

1 teaspoon dried parsley

½ teaspoon dried oregano

½ teaspoon dried thyme

1 teaspoon fine sea salt

¼ teaspoon black pepper

¼ teaspoon sugar

¼ cup (60 ml) apple cider vinegar

¼ cup plus 2 tablespoons (90 ml) olive oil

**FOR SANDWICHES**

Four 6-inch (15-cm) hoagie rolls,
cut in half and toasted

8 thin Mushroom Tomato Slices (page 183)

8 thin Gobbler Slices (page 182)

2 tomatoes, sliced into ½-inch (1.3-cm) rounds

6 cups (420 g) shredded lettuce

1 sweet onion, sliced, cut into half-moons, and separated

**TO MAKE THE DRESSING:** Combine the herbs, seasonings, sugar, and vinegar in a small bowl. Whisk to combine, then let soften for 5 minutes before adding the oil. Whisk the oil into the dressing.

**TO ASSEMBLE THE SANDWICHES:** Pour about 1 tablespoon (15 ml) dressing on the bottom of each roll. Layer 2 slices of each cold cut per roll, folding them in half if they are much larger than the roll. Lay the tomatoes on top, and spread 1½ cups (105 g) lettuce on each. Divide the onion evenly among the rolls. Pour the remaining dressing over the tops of the sandwiches and put the tops on the rolls. Cut in half and serve.

**SERVING SUGGESTIONS AND VARIATIONS**

• Of course, this sandwich can be customized with your favorite additions, such as grilled onions and peppers, pickles, or banana peppers.

• To make these as toasted cheese grinders, sprinkle a little shredded nondairy cheese on the toasted hoagie rolls. Broil for 2 minutes or until melted. Add the fillings as above.

# DEVILED (NOT) EGG SALAD SANDWICHES

Packed with flavor and personality, this one is sure to be a hit even for those who never were such big fans of egg salad. We adore the crunch and saltiness the (optional, but not in our world) pretzels bring to the table!

**YIELD**
2 OR 3 SANDWICHES

## FOR FILLING

2 cups (328 g) cooked chickpeas

2 tablespoons (30 ml) fresh lemon juice

1 tablespoon (15 ml) tamari

½ teaspoon liquid smoke

2 tablespoons (15 g) nutritional yeast

¼ teaspoon turmeric

3 tablespoons (42 g) vegan mayonnaise, plus extra if needed

1 teaspoon sweet pickle relish

1 teaspoon Dijon mustard

½ teaspoon capers, drained

1 tablespoon (10 g) minced onion

1 tablespoon (9 g) minced red bell pepper

1 teaspoon minced fresh parsley

¼ teaspoon smoked paprika

Salt and pepper, to taste

## FOR SANDWICHES

4 to 6 slices Green Monster Bread (page 178) or any bread

½ cup (16 g) fresh baby spinach

1 firm tomato, sliced

Pretzel sticks (optional)

**TO MAKE THE FILLING:** In a large skillet, combine the chickpeas, lemon juice, tamari, liquid smoke, nutritional yeast, and turmeric. Stir to coat the chickpeas. Cook over medium heat until the liquid has evaporated and the chickpeas are coated, about 6 minutes. Combine the remaining ingredients in a medium-size bowl. Add the chickpeas, stirring well to coat. Partially crush the chickpeas so they don't roll out of the bread as you eat them. Adjust the seasonings to taste and add more mayo, if desired. Chill for a couple of hours before using.

**TO ASSEMBLE THE SANDWICHES:** Spread ½ to ¾ cup (110 to 165 g) filling on the bread. The quantity will depend on your personal taste. (We like to overfill this one!) Top with the spinach, tomato, and a small handful of pretzel sticks for added crunch.

### SERVING SUGGESTIONS AND VARIATIONS

Not in a chickpea mood? Make it with tofu instead. Use 12 ounces (340 g) extra-firm tofu, drained and pressed really well, then cut into ¼-inch (6-mm) cubes. Heat a large skillet over medium heat and spray with nonstick cooking spray. Add the tofu cubes, cooking until golden brown and stirring occasionally, about 5 to 7 minutes. Follow the instructions for the filling from this point on.

# FRENCH TOFU SALAD WITH GRAPES

With crunchy almonds and sweet grapes, this elegant tofu salad sandwich will have you oooh-la-la-ing. Using both fresh and dried herbs brings a complexity of flavor. It's a perfect picnic sandwich and pairs wonderfully with a dry white vegan wine.

**YIELD**
4 SANDWICHES

**FOR TOFU SALAD**

1 teaspoon canola oil, if needed

1 pound (454 g) extra-firm tofu, drained, pressed, and cut into ½-inch (1.3-cm) cubes

1 teaspoon tamari

¼ cup (56 g) vegan mayonnaise

¼ cup (37 g) quartered seedless green grapes

2 tablespoons (20 g) minced shallot

1 tablespoon (15 g) minced celery

1 tablespoon (15 ml) white wine vinegar

1 tablespoon (7 g) slivered almonds, toasted

1 teaspoon minced fresh chives

½ teaspoon Dijon mustard

½ teaspoon minced fresh thyme

½ teaspoon minced fresh parsley

¼ teaspoon dried tarragon, crumbled

¼ teaspoon dried herbes de Provence

Salt and pepper, to taste

**FOR SANDWICHES**

1 cup (20 g) arugula, for serving

One 16-inch (40-cm) baguette, cut in half lengthwise

**TO MAKE THE TOFU SALAD:** Heat a large cast-iron skillet over medium heat. If the skillet is well seasoned, no oil is needed. If it isn't, add the canola oil. Add the tofu cubes and cook, pressing down with a spatula and stirring, for 7 to 8 minutes, or until lightly golden and a firmer texture. Remove from the heat and add the tamari. Transfer to a medium-size bowl. Add all the remaining ingredients and season to taste. Cover and refrigerate for 1 hour to let the flavors meld.

**TO ASSEMBLE THE SANDWICHES:** Place the arugula on the bottom of the baguette. Spread the tofu salad evenly over the arugula and top with the other half of the bread. Cut into 4 pieces and serve.

**SERVING SUGGESTIONS AND VARIATIONS**

• Instead of grapes, try substituting an equal amount of dried sweetened cranberries, dried cherries, minced fresh apples, or even raisins.

• For a change of pace, serve this on top of mixed greens for a take on a Waldorf salad.

# ALMO-CADO SANDWICHES

We grew tired of carrots always being number one in the world of shredded roots, so we decided to put the oft-ignored beet back in the spotlight, right where it belongs. This happily earthy sandwich is made a bit more substantial (not to mention delicious) thanks to the healthy fats naturally found in the almond butter and avocado. Applause!

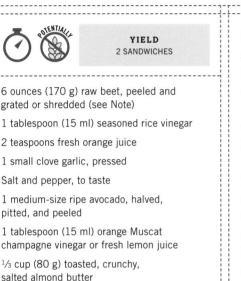

**YIELD**
2 SANDWICHES

6 ounces (170 g) raw beet, peeled and grated or shredded (see Note)

1 tablespoon (15 ml) seasoned rice vinegar

2 teaspoons fresh orange juice

1 small clove garlic, pressed

Salt and pepper, to taste

1 medium-size ripe avocado, halved, pitted, and peeled

1 tablespoon (15 ml) orange Muscat champagne vinegar or fresh lemon juice

⅓ cup (80 g) toasted, crunchy, salted almond butter

4 large slices whole-grain bread

½ cup (13 g) micro greens or (20 g) packed fresh herb salad mix

½ cup (17 g) onion sprouts or any spicy sprouts

Squeeze the liquid out of the grated beets if needed. This step shouldn't be necessary if you're shredding the beets. In a medium-size bowl, combine the beets with the vinegar, orange juice, and garlic. Add salt and pepper to taste.

Cut the avocado into thin slices and gently rub the slices with the Muscat vinegar to boost the flavor and prevent browning.

To assemble the sandwiches, spread 1½ tablespoons (24 g) almond butter on each slice of bread, or enough to cover the entire surface of the slices. Lightly drop some of the micro greens and sprouts on two slices, keeping a little aside. Arrange half of the grated beets on top, along with half of the sliced avocado and the remaining micro greens and sprouts. Add a little extra salt and pepper, if desired. Top with the other almond-buttered slice of bread.

### RECIPE NOTE

The finer you grate the beets, the more liquid will be released, making it so you'll have to squeeze the grated beets before adding them to the sandwich to avoid sogginess. Shredding them a bit thicker eliminates this step, so take your pick depending on the texture you prefer.

### SERVING SUGGESTIONS AND VARIATIONS

• Enjoy this sandwich with a side of crispy sweet potato chips to make it an even more special treat.

• If your bread is on the soft side, lightly toast it before assembling the sandwich; it'll be all the better for it.

• Choose a type of bread that has some character and texture to it (with seeds and nuts, perhaps), and avoid plain sandwich bread.

# RADISH AND CREAMY CHEESE BAGEL SANDWICHES

When it's hot and humid, we want to heat up our kitchens as little as possible. The toaster, we can do! This one hits the spot and won't overheat you or your home. The slightly salty, slightly sweet cream cheese mixture pairs beautifully with crisp radishes and peppery arugula.

**YIELD**
4 SANDWICHES

¾ cup (180 g) nondairy cream cheese, softened

¼ cup (40 g) minced shallot

1 tablespoon (3 g) minced chives

1 tablespoon (9 g) minced raisins

2 teaspoons ume plum vinegar

Pinch of black pepper

4 bagels, sliced and toasted

4 large radishes, sliced

1 cup (20 g) baby arugula

In a small bowl, combine the cream cheese, shallot, chives, raisins, vinegar, and black pepper. Mix with a fork until combined. Spread 1 tablespoon (15 g) on the inside of each of the toasted bagel tops. Divide the remaining 2 tablespoons (30 g) among the bagel bottoms. Layer the sliced radishes evenly over the bagel bottoms. Top with ¼ cup (5 g) arugula and the top of the bagel. Serve.

**SERVING SUGGESTIONS AND VARIATIONS**

• Add any other vegetables you like. Sliced bell pepper rings are a particularly good addition.

• If you have a favorite gazpacho, this recipe is the perfect side.

• This cheese mixture makes a unique base for bruschetta toppings. Spread it thinly on toasted baguette slices and top with tomatoes, basil, and garlic or the toppings of your choice.

# APPLE RADICCHIO NUTTY SANDWICHES

Crunchiness, crispiness, and creaminess, ahoy! We're not that big on processed, store-bought items and tried to limit their use in this book, but we haven't come up with the perfect home-made version of nondairy cream cheese to this day. We're sure we'll crack the code eventually, mark our words.

**YIELD**
4 SANDWICHES
1¼ CUPS (300 G)
NUTTY CREAM CHEESE

2 tablespoons (30 ml) thawed apple juice concentrate

2 tablespoons (12 g) grated daikon radish

1 tablespoon (10 g) minced shallot, divided

1 teaspoon apple cider vinegar or sherry vinegar

1 teaspoon Dijon mustard

Salt and pepper, to taste

1 medium-size Granny Smith apple, not peeled, cored and chopped

8 ounces (227 g) nondairy cream cheese, softened

⅔ cup (66 g) toasted pecan pieces

8 pumpernickel bread slices

8 radicchio leaves

1 cup (20 g) fresh baby arugula

Combine the apple juice concentrate, grated daikon, 2 teaspoons of the minced shallot, vinegar, mustard, salt, and pepper in a medium-size bowl. Add the chopped apple and stir well. Set aside at room temperature for 30 minutes to let the flavors meld.

In a medium-size bowl, combine the cream cheese, pecans, a pinch of salt and pepper, and the remaining 1 teaspoon minced shallot, using a couple of spoons to thoroughly incorporate the pecans into the softened cream cheese without crushing them.

Spread 2 tablespoons (30 g) nutty cream cheese on each slice of bread. Top with 2 radicchio leaves, ¼ cup (5 g) arugula, ¼ cup (35 g) apple salad, and the remaining slice of bread.

**SERVING SUGGESTIONS AND VARIATIONS**

• If you're not a fan of pumpernickel, you can switch to another bread, but be sure to choose one that's got some oomph and mucho flavor to it, something preferably whole grain that will bring some attitude to the sandwich table.

• We love to eat this one with a big handful of good old salted potato chips. Can't get enough of that crunch!

• If you're feeling a bit lazy or rushed, skip the daikon preparation and just add thin slices of Granny Smith apple to the pumpernickel already garnished with the cream cheese and pecan spread, and top with a few salad leaves for good measure.

# RAZZ-ELNUT SPINACH SANDWICHES

When we came across a recipe for a sandwich spread that combined regular mayonnaise with raspberries, we were a little intrigued by it, and yet not quite sold on how the flavors would pair up. We came up with our own (vegan, of course) version of it and fell in love with the pink hue and tingling flavor of this new favorite spread!

**YIELD**
4 SANDWICHES

### FOR RASPBERRY SPREAD

¼ cup (47 g) frozen raspberries, thawed and drained

½ cup (120 g) miso dressing (page 107)

1½ teaspoons minced shallot

Generous ¼ teaspoon fresh thyme leaves, chopped

### FOR SANDWICHES

4 bagels or any soft bread roll, cut in half and lightly toasted

⅓ cup (38 g) coarsely chopped dry-roasted hazelnuts

2 cups (57 g) baby spinach

32 super-thin Gobbler Slices (page 182)

**TO MAKE THE SPREAD:** Combine all the ingredients in a small bowl, making sure that no large pieces of raspberries are left.

**TO ASSEMBLE THE SANDWICHES:** Spread 1 heaping table-spoon (16 g) raspberry spread on each bagel half (or enough to cover the surface of it). Top with 1 heaping tablespoon (10 g) chopped hazelnuts. Cover with ½ cup (14 g) baby spinach, 8 Gobbler Slices, and the other bagel half.

### SERVING SUGGESTIONS AND VARIATIONS

- If you do prepare this one ahead of time for travel, be sure to add the spinach leaves between the bagel and the spread to help prevent sogginess.

- There will be some leftover spread, and though we've been known to occasionally just grab a spoon and eat it as one would eat yogurt (it's that good, don't judge us), we recommend spreading it on toasted bagel halves in place of nondairy cream cheese.

# TOFU POMEGRANATE POCKETS

Savory tofu bits combine with pomegranate to make a palate-pleasing pita sandwich. The pomegranate seeds add texture and a tart sweetness, while the ume plum vinegar brings it all together.

| YIELD |
| --- |
| 4 HALF POCKETS |

**FOR TOFU BITS**

Nonstick cooking spray

1 pound (454 g) extra-firm tofu, drained, pressed, and cut into ½-inch (1.3-cm) cubes

2 tablespoons (30 ml) tamari

1½ teaspoons liquid smoke, divided

1 teaspoon pure maple syrup

½ teaspoon onion powder

½ teaspoon fine sea salt

¼ teaspoon ground black pepper

**FOR DRESSING**

½ cup (69 g) cashews, soaked in water for 1 hour, then rinsed and drained

¼ cup plus 2 tablespoons (90) apple juice, or as needed

1 tablespoon plus 1 teaspoon (20 ml) ume plum vinegar

**FOR SANDWICHES**

4 cups (120 g) chopped baby spinach or arugula

¼ cup (40 g) minced red onion

Two 8-inch (20-cm) pita breads, cut in half

1 small cucumber, sliced

½ cup (91 g) pomegranate seeds, divided

**TO MAKE THE TOFU:** Preheat the oven to 400°F (200°C, or gas mark 6). Spray an 8 x 11-inch (20 x 28-cm) pan with nonstick spray. Combine the tofu, tamari, 1 teaspoon of the liquid smoke, maple syrup, onion powder, salt, and pepper in the pan. Stir to coat. Bake for 20 minutes, stirring once halfway through. When browned, remove from the oven and add the remaining ½ teaspoon liquid smoke. Let cool before using.

**TO MAKE THE DRESSING:** Combine all the ingredients in a blender. Blend until completely smooth.

**TO ASSEMBLE THE SANDWICHES:** Combine the spinach, red onion, and half the dressing in a bowl. Toss to coat. Fill the pockets evenly with the salad and then layer in the cucumber. Fill evenly with the tofu and sprinkle each with 2 tablespoons (23 g) pomegranate seeds. Drizzle with the remaining dressing and serve.

**SERVING SUGGESTIONS AND VARIATIONS**

Want to take this one on the go? You can toss all the sandwich vegetables with the dressing and package it separately from the tofu. When you're ready to eat, just fill the pitas with the salad and tofu.

# TEMPEH ARUGULA CAESAR WRAPS

Classic Caesar salad was never our thing. So we took the very best parts of it and created a wrap showcasing seasoned tempeh strips, a lovely green salad, and the quintessential "hippie" food: sunflower seeds.

| YIELD |
|---|
| 4 WRAPS |

## FOR SALAD DRESSING

¼ cup (34 g) cashews, soaked in water for 1 hour, then rinsed and drained

2 tablespoons (30 ml) capers, with brine

2 tablespoons (30 ml) red wine vinegar

2 tablespoons (30 ml) nondairy milk

2 tablespoons (30 ml) olive oil

1 tablespoon plus 1 teaspoon (20 ml) fresh lemon juice

2 cloves garlic, minced

2 teaspoons nutritional yeast

½ teaspoon agave nectar

½ teaspoon black pepper

1 teaspoon minced chives

## FOR TEMPEH AND SANDWICHES

1 pound (454 g) tempeh, steamed and cut into ½-inch (1.3-cm) slices

2 tablespoons (30 ml) tamari

Canola or other vegetable oil, for frying

½ teaspoon salt

¼ teaspoon black pepper

4 cups (80 g) chopped arugula

2 cups (94 g) chopped romaine

2 cups (360 g) chopped roasted red bell pepper

½ cup (80 g) minced red onion

Four 10-inch (25-cm) flour tortillas

2 tablespoons (9 g) sunflower seeds

1 tomato, sliced

**TO MAKE THE SALAD DRESSING:** In a blender, combine the cashews, capers and brine, vinegar, milk, oil, lemon juice, garlic, nutritional yeast, agave, and black pepper. Blend until smooth. Stir in the chives. Store in an airtight container in the refrigerator for up to 1 week.

**TO MAKE THE TEMPEH:** On a large baking sheet, combine the tempeh strips with the tamari. Let sit for 30 minutes, or until the tamari has been absorbed.

Preheat the oven to 250°F (120°C, or gas mark ½). Line a baking sheet with a paper towel. Pour ¼ inch (6 mm) oil into a large cast-iron skillet and heat over medium heat. Working in batches, panfry the tempeh, turning once, for 10 minutes, or until golden. Transfer to the baking sheet and keep warm in the oven. When all the tempeh is cooked, season with the salt and pepper. In a large bowl, combine the arugula, romaine, red pepper, and onion. Add the dressing and toss to coat.

**TO ASSEMBLE THE SANDWICHES:** Divide the tempeh evenly among the 4 tortillas. Top each with one-fourth of the salad mixture, sunflower seeds, and sliced tomato. Fold the ends in and roll. Cut in half to serve.

### SERVING SUGGESTIONS AND VARIATIONS

• Instead of serving these as wraps, make them as pita pocket sandwiches.

• We know this is a sandwich book, but we're just going to come out and say it. The dressed vegetables, topped with the tempeh, make a delicious salad.

# BULGUR HUMMUS WRAPS

One of our favorite grocery stores sells veggie wraps that are so irresistible we just had to try and re-create them at home!

**YIELD**
6 WRAPS

**FOR BULGUR**

½ cup (70 g) dry bulgur wheat

1 tablespoon (15 ml) fresh lemon juice

¼ cup plus 3 tablespoons (105 ml) water

¼ teaspoon fine sea salt, to taste

¼ teaspoon cayenne pepper, to taste

½ teaspoon onion powder

1 clove garlic, pressed

**FOR HUMMUS**

1 can (15 ounces, or 425 g) chickpeas, drained and rinsed

2 tablespoons (30 ml) olive oil

2 heaping tablespoons (40 g) tahini

2 tablespoons (30 ml) fresh lemon juice

1 tablespoon (15 ml) brine from jar of capers

½ teaspoon paprika

2 cloves garlic, pressed

Salt, to taste

2 tablespoons (15 g) capers

**FOR VEGGIES**

1 tablespoon (15 ml) olive oil

⅓ cup (50 g) chopped red onion

4 cups (209 g) mix of shredded green cabbage, red cabbage, and carrots

Salt and pepper, to taste

**FOR WRAPS**

1 tablespoon (15 ml) extra-virgin olive oil or fresh lemon juice

Six 10-inch (25-cm) flour tortillas

**TO MAKE THE BULGUR:** Combine all the ingredients in a medium-size bowl. Cover with plastic wrap and place in the fridge for 2 hours, until the liquid has been absorbed. Fluff with a fork. Set aside.

**TO MAKE THE HUMMUS:** Combine the chickpeas, olive oil, tahini, lemon juice, brine, paprika, garlic, and salt in a food processor. Process until mostly smooth, scraping down the sides with a rubber spatula. Add the capers and pulse a few times, just so the capers are partially chopped.

**TO MAKE THE VEGGIES:** Heat the oil in a large skillet. Add the onion and shredded veggies and cook over medium-high heat for 6 minutes, stirring occasionally, until the veggies just start to soften. Remove from the heat, add a pinch of salt and pepper, add to the bulgur, and stir to combine. Let cool completely.

**TO ASSEMBLE THE WRAPS:** Stir the oil into the cooled bulgur mix. Spread ¼ cup (63 g) hummus onto each wrap. Add ⅓ cup (50 g) bulgur mix on top and roll up tightly, tucking in the ends midway through rolling. Cut in half and serve.

**RECIPE NOTE**

Forget about overcooked bulgur! Soaking the grain to plump it up works quickly and yields perfect results every time.

**SERVING SUGGESTIONS AND VARIATIONS**

• We like to dip these wraps in tahini dressing (page 131).

• If you want to keep the cooking to a minimum, just nix the oil the veggies would have been cooked in, halve the quantity of cabbage mix and onion, and use them raw by combining them, along with the salt and pepper, with the "cooked" bulgur.

# INSIDE-OUT RICE-ADILLA

This is a terrific way to use leftover rice. Packed with fresh vegetables, rice, and Mexican spices, these can be on the table in no time. For the hot sauce, we prefer Frank's Original, if available.

**YIELD**
4 SERVINGS

**FOR RICE-ADILLAS**

1 tablespoon (15 ml) olive oil

½ cup (80 g) minced red onion

1 cup (100 g) chopped cauliflower florets

½ minced jalapeño, to taste

1 teaspoon ground cumin

1½ cups (237 g) cooked rice, chilled

2 cups (72 g) shredded Swiss chard, stems discarded

2 cloves garlic, minced

1 tablespoon (15 ml) hot sauce, to taste

Salt and pepper, to taste

Four 10-inch (25-cm) flour tortillas

**FOR BEAN TOPPING**

1 can (15 ounces, or 425 g) kidney beans, drained and rinsed

1 cup (130 g) jicama matchsticks

½ cup (50 g) minced scallion

2 tablespoons (2 g) minced fresh cilantro

1 tablespoon (15 ml) apple cider vinegar

1 tablespoon (15 ml) fresh lime juice

1 tablespoon (15 ml) hot sauce, to taste

Salt and pepper, to taste

**FOR SERVING**

1 avocado, pitted, peeled, and sliced

Hot sauce

**TO MAKE THE RICE-ADILLAS:** Heat the oil in a large skillet over medium heat. Add the onion, cauliflower, jalapeño, and cumin and cook for 3 minutes. Add the rice, Swiss chard, and garlic. Cook until just wilting, 3 to 4 minutes. Add the hot sauce and season to taste with salt and pepper.

Preheat a panini press fitted with smooth plates on high. Divide the mixture evenly between 2 tortillas. Top with the remaining 2 tortillas. Place on the press and close. Cook for 4 to 5 minutes, or until golden and crisp. Cut each tortilla into quarters.

**TO MAKE THE TOPPING:** Combine all the ingredients in a medium-size bowl. Stir to combine and adjust the seasonings to taste.

Place 2 tortilla quarters on each of 4 plates and top with ¾ cup (106 g) bean topping. Serve with the avocado slices and extra hot sauce.

---

**SERVING SUGGESTIONS AND VARIATIONS**

• No panini press? Preheat the oven to 400°F (200°C, or gas mark 6). Lightly coat a baking sheet with nonstick spray. Place the filled quesadillas on the sheet and lightly spray the tops with nonstick spray. Bake for 5 to 7 minutes, or until crisp. Cut into wedges and serve.

• If you're short on time, feel free to omit the bean topping. Serve with salsa or guacamole (or both!) instead.

# SUSHI SOY WRAPS

If sushi grew up and turned into a full-fledged sandwich, this would be it! Crispy tempura is accented by pickled vegetables, creamy avocado, and sushi rice. The sauce combines sweet, sour, salty, and bitter to tempt your taste buds with umami, making this sandwich exceptional.

**YIELD**
4 WRAPS

1 cup (145 g) prepared, sushi rice

¾ cup (180 ml) water

1 tablespoon (15 ml) seasoned rice vinegar

½ teaspoon tamari

¼ teaspoon toasted sesame oil

Pinch of sugar

**FOR GINGERY VEGETABLES**

1½ cups (225 g) shredded napa cabbage

½ cup (48 g) grated daikon radish

½ cup (50 g) chopped scallion

2 teaspoons ume plum vinegar

½ teaspoon grated fresh ginger

**FOR DIPPING SAUCE**

2 tablespoons (30 ml) mirin

½ teaspoon sriracha, to taste

½ teaspoon tamari

½ teaspoon ume plum vinegar

**FOR TEMPURA**

¾ cup (94 g) all-purpose flour

½ teaspoon fine sea salt

¼ teaspoon baking powder

⅔ cup (160 ml) sparkling water, chilled

Canola oil, for cooking

6 asparagus stalks, cut in half

1 large portobello mushroom cap, stemmed, gilled, and cut into ½-inch (1.3-cm) slices

**FOR WRAPS**

4 soy wraps

½ avocado, pitted, peeled, and sliced

**TO MAKE THE RICE:** Combine the rice and water and cook according to the package directions. Scoop it into a bowl. Combine the vinegar, tamari, oil, and sugar in a small bowl, then pour over the rice and gently fluff. Let cool.

**TO MAKE THE VEGETABLES:** Stir all the ingredients together in a medium-size bowl.

**TO MAKE THE DIPPING SAUCE:** Combine all the ingredients in a small bowl.

**TO MAKE THE TEMPURA:** Whisk the flour, salt, and baking powder together in a deep bowl. Whisk in the sparkling water. The mixture should be thick enough to coat the asparagus and mushroom without dripping off. If needed, add 1 tablespoon (8 g) flour or (15 ml) sparkling water.

Line a baking sheet with paper towels. Pour 1 to 2 inches (2.5 to 5 cm) canola oil into a deep, heavy-bottomed saucepan, and heat over medium-high heat. Or heat 3 to 4 inches (7.5 to 10 cm) oil in a deep fryer to medium-high heat. Working in batches, dip the vegetables in the batter to coat, slide them into the oil, and fry until golden, 4 to 5 minutes. Do not crowd the fryer or the temperature of the oil will drop. The correct oil temperature should cause a coated vegetable to bubble. Batter and fry all the vegetables and transfer them to the baking sheet to drain.

**TO ASSEMBLE THE WRAPS:** Place the wraps on a cutting board. In the center, spread ¼ cup (46 g) rice and ¼ cup (20 g) vegetables. Top evenly with the tempura and the avocado slices. Fold two opposite corners in and roll the wrap closed. Serve with the dipping sauce.

# PROTEIN-HAPPY QUINOA WRAPS

Super-packed with protein, courtesy of the quinoa and beans, this Mediterranean-inspired roll will fill you with such tremendous energy that you'll keep hacking away at the day's chores without ever wanting or needing to stop. Okay, slight exaggeration, but just barely.

**YIELD**
4 WRAPS, GENEROUS ¾ CUP
(100 G) TAPENADE

**FOR TAPENADE**

½ cup (28 g) minced sun-dried tomatoes
(moist vacuum-packed, not oil-packed)

¼ cup (25 g) minced kalamata olives

2 tablespoons (15 g) chopped capers

2 tablespoons (30 ml) olive oil

¼ teaspoon red pepper flakes

**FOR FILLING**

1½ cups (355 ml) vegetable broth

½ cup (84 g) dry quinoa

¼ cup (30 g) packed golden raisins (optional)

1 tablespoon (15 ml) apple cider vinegar

1 tablespoon (15 ml) fresh lemon juice

1½ tablespoons (25 ml) olive oil

¼ teaspoon red pepper flakes, to taste

1½ tablespoons (15 g) minced red onion

1 clove garlic, minced

Fine sea salt, to taste

Cracked black pepper, to taste

2 tablespoons (15 g) roasted salted pepitas

¾ cup (197 g) cooked cannellini beans

2 tablespoons (8 g) chopped fresh parsley

1 tablespoon (2 g) minced fresh basil

**FOR WRAPS**

Four 10-inch (25-cm) flour tortillas

1 red bell pepper, cored and cut into strips

1 small cucumber, cut into strips

**TO MAKE THE TAPENADE:** Combine all the ingredients in a food processor. Pulse a few times, but leave it chunky. Chill for at least 2 hours to let the flavors develop.

**TO MAKE THE QUINOA:** Bring the broth to a boil in a medium-size pot. Add the quinoa and cook for 8 minutes. Add the raisins and cook for 2 to 4 minutes longer, or until the quinoa is cooked and the telltale tail appears. Drain in a fine-mesh sieve. Set aside to cool completely.

In the meantime, prepare the dressing by combining the vinegar, lemon juice, oil, red pepper flakes, onion, garlic, salt, pepper, pepitas, and beans in a large bowl. Add the quinoa mixture, parsley, and basil to the dressing and stir until well coated.

**TO ASSEMBLE THE WRAPS:** In the middle of each wrap, spread 3 tablespoons (25 g) tapenade. Top with a generous $1/2$ cup (120 g) quinoa filling. Divide the red bell pepper and cucumber among the wraps. Fold the ends in and roll closed.

# MANGO BASIL WRAPS

Crunchy veggies paired with exotic flavors make this spicy wrap especially handy (both literally and figuratively, as a matter of fact) during the sweltering hot summer months.

**YIELD**
6 WRAPS
2 CUPS (800 G) SPREAD

## FOR COCONUT SPREAD

1 package (7 ounces, or 200 g) creamed coconut (see page 13)

1 cup (235 ml) warm water

2 tablespoons (30 ml) fresh lemon juice

2 teaspoons onion powder

2 cloves garlic, to taste

½ teaspoon fine sea salt, to taste

½ teaspoon red pepper flakes

1 teaspoon ground ginger

½ teaspoon coarse black pepper

## FOR WRAPS

Six 10-inch (25-cm) flour tortillas

2 ounces (57 g) snow pea sprouts or shoots or favorite sprouts

1 large English cucumber, thinly sliced

1 large, not overly ripe mango, peeled, pitted, and cut into cubes

3 small avocados, pitted, peeled, and sliced (optional)

24 fresh basil leaves

Salt and pepper, to taste

6 tablespoons (6 g) chopped fresh cilantro or parsley

**TO MAKE THE SPREAD:** Combine all the ingredients in a blender, and blend until smooth. Place in the fridge for 1 to 2 hours, stirring occasionally to check on thickness. It will thicken and set as it chills. If the spread is too thick upon coming out of the fridge, reheat it just for a few seconds in the microwave or leave it at room temperature until it is spreadable. You will have extra spread left over; store it in an airtight container in the fridge and save for another use. (To use it as a sauce in other recipes, reheat it in the microwave or in a saucepan over low heat.)

**TO ASSEMBLE THE WRAPS:** Smear 2 tablespoons (50 g) coconut spread in the center of each tortilla. Place a generous handful of sprouts on top, followed by ⅓ cup (34 g) cucumber, ¼ cup (41 g) mango, the slices of ½ an avocado, and 4 basil leaves. Sprinkle with a little salt and pepper to taste, and top it off with 1 tablespoon (1 g) cilantro. Wrap tightly and serve.

### SERVING SUGGESTIONS AND VARIATIONS

- If you are craving some protein, add a small handful of black beans or panfried tofu cubes. Prepare the Tofu Bits (page 67), dropping the liquid smoke and maple syrup from the list of ingredients in this application.

- While we like to simply slather the coconut spread on slices of bread like we would vegan cream cheese or butter, we also think it's swell to heat it and use it as a sauce over cooked brown jasmine rice or any kind of bean for a satisfyingly easy, filling meal on the go.

# CAJUN LETTUCE WRAPS

Ramen noodles, a mainstay of youth for many, get special treatment here. The Cajun "trinity" of vegetables enhances our well-seasoned and unique take on an Asian favorite. These are best served at room temperature. If you're a fan of spice, feel free to add ¼ to ½ teaspoon cayenne pepper to the bean mixture when adding the spices.

**YIELD**
8 LETTUCE WRAPS

2 teaspoons olive oil

½ cup (80 g) minced onion

⅓ cup (33 g) green beans, cut into pieces ½ inch (1.3 cm) long

¼ cup (38 g) minced green bell pepper

2 tablespoons (16 g) minced celery

1 teaspoon paprika

½ teaspoon dried thyme

½ teaspoon dried oregano

½ teaspoon fine sea salt

¼ teaspoon black pepper

2 cloves garlic, minced

1 can (15 ounces, or 425 g) red or kidney beans, drained and rinsed

¾ cup (108 g) fresh or frozen corn, rinsed

2 tablespoons (33 g) tomato paste

¼ cup (60 ml) vegetable broth

2 packages (2 ounces, or 60 g each) dried ramen noodles, broken, seasoning packets discarded

1 tablespoon (15 ml) hot sauce, plus more for serving

⅓ cup (30 g) minced scallion, plus more for garnish

16 large Boston, Bibb, or butter lettuce leaves

¼ cup (35 g) chopped dry-roasted peanuts

Heat the oil in a large skillet over medium heat. Add the onion, green beans, green pepper, and celery and cook for 2 to 3 minutes. Add the paprika, thyme, oregano, salt, black pepper, and garlic. Cook, stirring occasionally, for 3 to 4 minutes, or until fragrant. Add the beans, corn, tomato paste, and broth. Cook, stirring occasionally, for 5 minutes. If the mixture is too dry, add 1 tablespoon (15 ml) broth. Taste and adjust the seasonings. Set aside.

Cook the ramen noodles in boiling water for 4 minutes or according to package directions. Drain and run the noodles under cold water to stop the cooking. Return them to the saucepan and add the hot sauce and scallion. Stir to combine.

Layer 2 lettuce leaves on top of each other. In the center of each pair, place ¼ cup (67 g) noodles and a heaping ⅓ cup (57 g) bean mixture. Top with the peanuts and a few scallions for garnish. Serve with extra hot sauce on the side.

**SERVING SUGGESTIONS AND VARIATIONS**

These are easy to pack: Package the noodles, bean mixture, lettuce leaves, and garnish all independently. Assemble when ready to eat.

# WATERMELON MISO WRAPS

A summery wrap par excellence, this is yet another recipe that will become the Holy Grail of those unbearably muggy days, when you can hardly bear the thought of doing any cooking at all. It is also a creative way to put watermelon to good use instead of just biting into slices of the stuff. Not that there's anything wrong with that, but we're just saying.

**YIELD**
4 WRAPS
¾ CUP (180 ML) DRESSING

### FOR YOGURT DRESSING

3 tablespoons (45 g) unsweetened plain nondairy yogurt

3 tablespoons (45 ml) olive oil

2 to 3 tablespoons (30 to 45 ml) white balsamic vinegar, to taste

2 tablespoons (36 g) white miso

¼ teaspoon ground white or black pepper, to taste

### FOR WRAPS

Four 9-inch (23-cm) flour tortillas

1 cup (43 g) baby romaine

1 cup (43 g) baby arugula

1 cup (154 g) watermelon balls (see Note)

½ cup (62 g) dry-roasted salted pistachios, coarsely chopped

2 tablespoons (3 g) chopped fresh mint, to taste (optional)

4 razor-thin slices red onion

**TO MAKE THE DRESSING:** Whisk all the ingredients together in a medium-size bowl. Store in an airtight container in the fridge. The dressing will keep for up to 5 days.

**TO ASSEMBLE THE WRAPS:** Top each wrap with ¼ cup (11 g) baby romaine, ¼ cup (11 g) baby arugula, ¼ cup (39 g) watermelon balls, 2 tablespoons (16 g) chopped pistachios, 1½ teaspoons chopped mint, and 1 slice onion. Add at least 2 tablespoons (30 ml) dressing on top, or more if desired. Wrap tightly and serve.

### RECIPE NOTE

• To make watermelon balls, use a melon baller to scoop out the flesh from your fresh watermelon. Place the balls in a fine-mesh sieve on top of a large bowl and let drain in the fridge for several hours. Do not skip the draining step in this recipe because it makes a noticeable difference in the texture of the melon.

• If watermelon isn't available, you can use any other sort of melon: honeydew or cantaloupe work well here, too. Be sure to drain those thoroughly, as well.

# STRAWBERRY SPINACH TACOWICH

Chances are, you can't get enough of fresh, sweet, and fragrant strawberries when they first appear in early summer. But if you want to try something different than dipping them into vegan cream, we have just the thing for you in this colorful, easy to throw together meal.

**YIELD**
8 TACOWICHES
¾ CUP (180 G) DRESSING

**FOR DRESSING**

¼ cup (60 ml) olive oil

¼ cup (60 g) unsweetened plain nondairy yogurt

Pinch of salt

¼ teaspoon ground white pepper, to taste

¼ cup (60 ml) orange Muscat champagne vinegar

1½ tablespoons (15 g) minced shallot

3 tablespoons (22 g) finely chopped dry-roasted hazelnuts, plus more for garnish

**FOR TACOWICHES**

Eight 6-inch (15-cm) corn or wheat tortillas, or any tortillas

2 cups (67 g) baby spinach

16 small (1 inch, or 2.5 cm) strawberries (about 4 ounces, or 112 g), hulled and quartered

**TO MAKE THE DRESSING:** Combine the oil, yogurt, salt, pepper, vinegar, and shallot in a blender and pulse until combined. Transfer to an airtight container and stir in the hazelnuts before sealing. Stored in the fridge, the dressing will keep for up to 4 days.

**TO ASSEMBLE THE TACOWICHES:** Spread 1 tablespoon (15 g) dressing onto each tortilla. Add ¼ cup (8 g) baby spinach, 2 quartered strawberries, and a sprinkling of chopped hazelnuts on top. Drizzle with extra dressing, if desired. Fold in half in true taco fashion to eat.

**SERVING SUGGESTIONS AND VARIATIONS**

- You ate a big meal for lunch and you're not in the mood for extra carbohydrates tonight? We understand. We occasionally feel that way, too. Rest assured that the filling of these tacos makes for a colorful and simple standalone salad. (Don't tell anyone we said that, since this is a sandwich book and all.)

- If you cannot find orange Muscat champagne vinegar, replace it with 3 tablespoons (45 ml) white balsamic vinegar, combined with 2 teaspoons orange juice and 1 teaspoon agave nectar.

# ORANGE FENNEL SUMMER ROLLS

Always fancy and refreshing, these summer rolls are an ideal option to keep things light for your next meal. They're perfect to make the night before and take on the go for lunch because of their lack of sogginess susceptibility.

**POTENTIALLY**

**YIELD**
16 SUMMER ROLLS

### FOR DIPPING SAUCE

2 tablespoons (30 ml) sesame oil

2 tablespoons (30 ml) seasoned rice vinegar

1 tablespoon (15 ml) fresh orange juice

1 teaspoon ground ginger

1 clove garlic, pressed

¼ teaspoon fine sea salt, to taste

¼ teaspoon red pepper flakes, to taste

### FOR ROLLS

16 rice paper wraps

2 cups (175 g) thinly sliced fennel (about 10 ounces, or 280 g untrimmed)

1 can (11 ounces, or 312 g) mandarin orange slices, drained

2 teaspoons black sesame seeds

**TO MAKE THE DIPPING SAUCE:** Whisk all the ingredients together in a medium-size bowl. Set aside.

**TO ASSEMBLE THE ROLLS:** Immerse the rice paper 1 sheet at a time in warm water to soften. Soak for a few seconds, until pliable. Handle carefully because rice paper breaks easily. Drain on a clean kitchen towel before rolling. Add 2 tablespoons (11 g) fennel, 2 slices mandarin orange, and a pinch of black sesame seeds. Roll tightly, folding the ends in and rolling closed. Serve with the dipping sauce. Store leftovers tightly wrapped in plastic in the fridge for up to 2 days.

### SERVING SUGGESTIONS AND VARIATIONS

- If you're no fennel fan, use the same quantity of napa cabbage instead of the fragrant bulb. In which case, you might want to consider adding ¼ cup (25 g) minced scallion to the chopped cabbage to make up for its subtler flavor.

- When you know you won't need these to be travel-friendly, use 4 large flour tortillas instead of rice paper wraps: simply add the fennel and orange slices on top of the tortilla, drizzle with the sauce, and sprinkle sesame seeds on top. Fold or wrap, and enjoy.

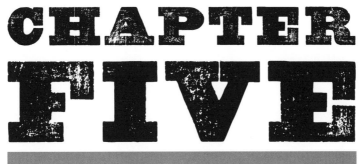

# CHAPTER FIVE

## THE CLASSICS & DELI DELIGHTS

{ **RETRO, DINER-STYLE SANDWICHES THAT WILL ROCK YOUR WORLD** }

Restaurants often build their reputations on these all-time favorites. Sadly, they're rarely vegan. But we've got you covered with regional favorites, stacked sandwiches, and even a little international flair. Just don't forget to tip or hug whoever cooks for you! (Even if it's yourself.)

◀ *The Almighty BLT*, page 86

# THE ALMIGHTY BLT

We decided to get rebellious here by saying no to plain mayo. The hearts of palm bring a little fiber and texture to the spread, which packs a lot of flavor and shines a whole new light on our veganized version of the beloved BLT *(pictured on page 84)*.

**YIELD**
4 SANDWICHES
2 CUPS (515 G) SPREAD

## FOR SPREAD

1 jar (14 ounces, or 392 g) hearts of palm, drained

¼ cup (60 g) nondairy sour cream or unsweetened plain nondairy yogurt

½ cup (112 g) vegan mayonnaise

¼ teaspoon ground white pepper, to taste

¼ teaspoon fine sea salt, to taste

1 tablespoon (8 g) drained capers

½ teaspoon red pepper flakes

1 teaspoon onion powder (optional)

2 cloves garlic, minced

2 tablespoons (14 g) sliced sun-dried tomatoes in oil, drained

## FOR SANDWICHES

8 slices any bread (crusty or soft), toasted

4 large lettuce leaves

1 recipe Tempeh Bacon (page 179), panfried

1 beefsteak tomato, cut into 8 thin slices

1 avocado, pitted, peeled, and cut into 12 slices

4 razor-thin slices red onion (optional)

**TO MAKE THE SPREAD:** Process the hearts of palm in a food processor until coarsely chopped. Add all the remaining ingredients and pulse a few times to leave chunky, or process thoroughly until smooth. Stop to scrape down the sides occasionally. Chill in an airtight container overnight to let the flavors meld. Enjoy the leftovers within 1 week.

**TO ASSEMBLE THE SANDWICHES:** Smear 1 tablespoon (16 g) spread on each slice of bread. Top 4 slices of bread with 1 lettuce leaf, 2 ounces (57 g) bacon, 2 slices tomato, 3 slices avocado, and 1 slice onion. Top with the 4 remaining bread slices.

### SERVING SUGGESTIONS AND VARIATIONS

• BLT sandwiches are commonly served with a side of French fries, but coleslaw or your favorite pickled vegetables will work well here if you really need something to accompany it. The sandwich alone usually hits the spot for us.

• Use the leftover spread as an alternative on any Mediterranean-style sandwich, such as the Ratatouille Sandwiches (page 102) and the Chazwich (page 151), to name but a few.

# ONE WORLD REUBEN

This classic sandwich is given a new twist thanks to the global flavors of harissa (from Tunisia), ume plum vinegar (from Japan), and garam masala (from India). Inspired by the Police song "One World," Tami thought it would be fun to create a global version of one of her all-time favorite sandwiches.

**YIELD**
4 SANDWICHES

**FOR SPREAD**

4 ounces (113 g) firm tofu, drained

1 tablespoon (10 g) minced onion

1 tablespoon (15 ml) dill pickle juice

2 teaspoons ume plum vinegar

2 teaspoons ketchup

1 teaspoon mustard

1 teaspoon harissa, to taste

1 tablespoon (15 g) sweet pickle relish

**FOR SEITAN**

1 pound (454 g) Moo-Free Seitan (page 180), thinly sliced

1½ teaspoons onion powder

¾ teaspoon mustard powder

¾ teaspoon garlic powder

¾ teaspoon garam masala

¼ teaspoon black pepper

¼ teaspoon fine sea salt

1 tablespoon (15 ml) canola oil

**FOR SANDWICHES**

¼ cup (56 g) nondairy butter

8 slices rye or swirl bread

3 cups (426 g) sauerkraut, drained and heated through, with a pinch of black pepper

1 tomato, thinly sliced

**TO MAKE THE SPREAD:** Combine the tofu, onion, pickle juice, vinegar, ketchup, mustard, and harissa in a blender. Blend until smooth. Stir in the relish. Transfer to an airtight container and refrigerate for at least 30 minutes.

**TO MAKE THE SEITAN:** Combine the seitan and spices in a 9 x 13-inch (23 x 33-cm) pan. Toss to coat the seitan. Heat the oil in a large skillet over medium-high heat. Cook the seitan for 5 minutes, stirring occasionally, until lightly browned.

**TO ASSEMBLE THE SANDWICHES:** Preheat a panini press fitted with smooth plates on high. Butter the outside of each slice of bread. Coat the inside of each slice of bread with 1 tablespoon (14 g) spread. Divide the seitan evenly among 4 slices. Top each with one-fourth of the sauerkraut and tomato slices. Put the tops on the sandwiches and grill with the press open for 5 minutes, or until golden. Carefully turn over and cook the other side for 3 to 4 minutes. Cut in half and serve.

**SERVING SUGGESTIONS AND VARIATIONS**

Sliced apples go so well with anything sauerkraut. When serving this, include some apples on the side.

# BIEROCKS

Reputed to be German, these stuffed buns have found a stronghold in the United States. Flavorful cabbage, tempeh, and sauerkraut are all wrapped in easy-to-make beer and caraway bread dough. Enjoy these at any temperature, topped with mustard. Serve with a green salad.

**YIELD**
8 BIEROCKS

### FOR FILLING

1½ cups (355 ml) vegetable broth

¼ cup (60 ml) red wine vinegar

2 tablespoons (33 g) tomato paste

1 tablespoon (15 ml) tamari

2 teaspoons onion powder

1 teaspoon cumin seeds

1 teaspoon paprika

½ teaspoon fennel seeds

½ teaspoon lemon pepper

2 cloves garlic, minced

1 teaspoon vegan Worcestershire sauce

8 ounces (227 g) tempeh, minced

2 tablespoons (30 ml) olive oil, divided

1 cup (160 g) minced onion

2 cups (180 g) chopped green cabbage

1 cup (142 g) sauerkraut, drained

⅓ cup (34 g) grated carrot

1 tablespoon (15 g) Dijon mustard

Salt and pepper, to taste

### FOR BUNS

3 cups (375 g) all-purpose flour

3 tablespoons (45 g) packed light brown sugar

2 teaspoons instant yeast

1 teaspoon fine sea salt

1 teaspoon caraway seeds

1 cup (235 ml) dark vegan beer, flat and at room temperature

Nondairy butter, for brushing

**TO MAKE THE FILLING:** In a medium-size saucepan, combine the broth, vinegar, tomato paste, tamari, onion powder, cumin seeds, paprika, fennel seeds, lemon pepper, garlic, and Worcestershire sauce. Bring to a boil, then reduce to a simmer and cook for 20 minutes. Place the tempeh and the marinade in an 8-inch (20-cm) pan. Marinate for 1 hour in the refrigerator.

Heat 1 tablespoon (15 ml) of the olive oil in a large skillet over medium heat. Drain the tempeh, reserving the marinade, and add to the pan. Cook, stirring, for 10 minutes. Remove the tempeh from the pan and set aside. Add the remaining 1 tablespoon (15 ml) oil, onion, and cabbage to the pan. Cook for 5 minutes. Add the sauerkraut, carrot, mustard, salt, pepper, tempeh, and reserved marinade. Cook, stirring, for 5 minutes. Let cool.

**TO MAKE THE BUNS:** Combine the flour, brown sugar, yeast, salt, caraway seeds, and beer in a medium-size bowl. Stir together. Knead for 8 minutes on a floured board. Add 1 tablespoon (8 g) flour or (15 ml) beer to make a workable dough. Form into a ball. Oil a large bowl. Place the dough in the bowl and cover with a towel. Let rise in a warm place for 1½ to 2 hours, or until doubled.

Evenly divide the dough into 8 pieces. On a floured surface, roll each into a 6-inch (15-cm) round. Scoop ½ cup (102 g) filling into the center and fold the sides in to seal. Pat the bun into a round and place seam-side down on a baking sheet. Repeat with the remaining dough. Let rise, covered with a towel, for 30 minutes.

Preheat the oven to 350°F (180°C, or gas mark 4).

Bake the buns for 30 minutes, or until golden. Brush with the melted butter. Transfer to a rack to cool. Serve warm or at room temperature.

# RACHEL SANDWICHES

The Rachel is a variation on the reuben. Sometimes it is served with traditional Thousand Island dressing, and other times with barbecue sauce. Almost always, coleslaw stands in for the sauerkraut. For our version, we dressed the slaw with Thousand Island, but couldn't resist adding the barbecue sauce, too.

**YIELD**
4 SANDWICHES

### FOR SEITAN

4 No Cluck Cutlets (page 181)

½ cup (120 ml) pickle juice

1 teaspoon caraway seeds, ground

1 teaspoon paprika

½ teaspoon fennel seeds, ground

½ teaspoon ground coriander

½ teaspoon fine sea salt

¼ teaspoon black pepper

½ cup (120 ml) vegetable broth

### FOR THOUSAND ISLAND COLESLAW

4 cups (280 g) shredded green cabbage

1 cup (70 g) shredded red cabbage

⅓ cup (55 g) minced red onion

⅓ cup (75 g) minced dill pickles

½ cup (112 g) vegan mayonnaise

2 tablespoons (30 g) ketchup

1 teaspoon mustard

½ teaspoon vegan Worcestershire sauce

½ to 1 teaspoon sriracha, to taste

Salt and pepper, to taste

### FOR SANDWICHES

4 slices rye bread, toasted

1 cup (250 g) Mac-Shroom barbecue sauce (page 123) or store-bought barbecue sauce, warmed

**TO MAKE THE SEITAN:** In a 9 x 13-inch (23 cm x 33-cm) pan, combine all the ingredients. Mix well. Let the seitan marinate in the refrigerator for 1 hour or longer.

Preheat the oven to 400°F (200°C, or gas mark 6). Bake the seitan for 15 minutes, turn over, and bake for 15 minutes longer, or until the marinade has been absorbed. Stack the cutlets on top of each other on a cutting board and slice thinly to form strips.

**TO MAKE THE SLAW:** In a medium-size bowl, stir together cabbages, onion, and pickles. In a small bowl, stir together mayonnaise, ketchup, mustard, Worcestershire, and sriracha. Add to the vegetables and toss to coat. Season to taste with salt and pepper.

**TO ASSEMBLE THE SANDWICHES:** Place a piece of toasted bread on each plate. Divide the seitan evenly among the sandwiches. Top with the barbecue sauce. Divide the coleslaw evenly on top of the sandwiches and serve.

**SERVING SUGGESTIONS AND VARIATIONS**

• Moo-Free Seitan (page 180), cut into strips, may be substituted for the No Cluck Cutlets.

• We like to serve this with carrot sticks and pepper strips on the side.

# CURRIED LENTIL WRAPS

When we warned the testers that this recipe offers a rather large yield, most of them prepared just half of it, only to regret not going for a full batch after having a taste of this spicy goodness. So let us warn you now: chances are, you will be hooked, too.

| YIELD |
|---|
| 8 TO 10 WRAPS |

## FOR CURRIED SAUCE

1 package (7 ounces, or 200 g) creamed coconut (see page 13)

1 cup (235 ml) warm water

2 tablespoons (30 ml) fresh lemon juice or apple cider vinegar

2 teaspoons onion powder

2 teaspoons curry powder

2 cloves garlic, to taste

½ teaspoon fine sea salt, to taste

½ teaspoon red pepper flakes

½ teaspoon ground ginger

## FOR LENTILS

1 cup (192 g) uncooked green or brown lentils

2 cups (470 ml) vegetable broth

2 cloves garlic, minced

¼ cup (36 g) golden raisins (optional)

2 teaspoons olive oil

½ cup (80 g) finely diced red onion

1 red bell pepper, cored and diced

Salt and pepper, to taste

## FOR WRAPS

Eight to ten 10-inch (25-cm) flour tortillas

**TO MAKE THE CURRIED SAUCE:** Combine all the ingredients in a blender and blend until smooth. Set aside.

**TO MAKE THE LENTILS:** Rinse the lentils and pick out any debris. Combine with the broth in a large pot and bring to a boil over high heat. Reduce the heat and simmer uncovered, checking for doneness after 20 minutes. Add ½ to 1 cup (120 to 235 ml) extra liquid if the lentils aren't tender enough by then and cook until the liquid is absorbed. The lentils should be toothsome, not mushy. Once the lentils are ready, add the curried sauce, garlic, and raisins and stir to combine. Set aside.

Place the oil in a large skillet. Heat over medium heat, add the onion and bell pepper, and cook until just softened, about 4 minutes. Add the lentils, season with salt and pepper to taste, and simmer for 5 minutes longer, until thickened but not dry.

**TO ASSEMBLE THE WRAPS:** Add about ½ cup (125 g) lentils to each tortilla. Fold the ends in and roll. Cut in half to serve.

### SERVING SUGGESTIONS AND VARIATIONS

• Because a meal can never contain too many vegetables, how about throwing 1½ cups (186 g) or more lightly steamed and chopped cauliflower into the sauced lentils before wrapping it all up? This might increase the total number of wraps by one or two, but we sincerely doubt anyone will complain.

• If you happen to have lentils that are already cooked, this will be a breeze to make and you will need 2½ cups (500 g) of them. Just combine the lentils with the curried sauce, garlic, and raisins, and then follow the rest of the instructions.

# FAUX-LAFEL

Instead of frying our falafel, we bake these for a lower-fat option. We're not claiming they are authentic, but we will say they're full of flavor. With the parts packed individually, this sandwich is ideal for on-the-go eating.

| YIELD |
|---|
| 4 SANDWICHES |

### FOR FALAFEL

2 cans (15 ounces, or 425 g each) chickpeas, drained and rinsed

¼ cup (40 g) minced onion

¼ cup (60 ml) fresh lemon juice

4 cloves garlic, minced

2 tablespoons (8 g) minced fresh parsley

2 teaspoons ground cumin

2 teaspoons ground coriander

2 teaspoons toasted sesame oil

¾ to 1 teaspoon red pepper flakes, to taste

½ teaspoon fine sea salt

Pinch of black pepper

2 teaspoons baking powder

2 to 3 tablespoons (16 to 24 g) all-purpose flour

1 tablespoon (15 ml) olive oil, for baking

### FOR SANDWICHES

Four 8-inch (20 cm) whole wheat pita breads, cut in half across

6 cups (420 g) shredded lettuce

2 large tomatoes, cut into ¼-inch (6-mm) slices

1 medium-size cucumber, cut into ⅛-inch (3-mm) slices

**TO MAKE THE FALAFEL:** Preheat the oven to 400°F (200°C, or gas mark 6). Oil a large baking sheet. In a medium-size bowl, combine the chickpeas, onion, lemon juice, garlic, parsley, cumin, coriander, sesame oil, red pepper flakes, salt, and pepper. Mash with a fork so that the chickpeas are broken into chunks but not to a paste. Add the baking powder and 2 tablespoons (16 g) of the flour. Mix well. Form a heaping tablespoon of the mixture into a patty 2 inches (5 cm) wide and ½ inch (1.3 cm) thick. If the patty does not hold together, add the remaining 1 tablespoon (8 g) flour. Place the patty on the baking sheet and repeat with the remaining dough. You should have 20 falafel patties. Brush them with the olive oil and bake for 15 minutes, or until the bottoms are golden. Turn and cook the other side for 8 minutes, or until golden.

**FOR TAHINI SAUCE:** Soak ¼ cup (32 g) cashews in water for 1 hour. Drain and rinse. Combine the cashews, 3 to 4 tablespoons (45 to 60 ml) nondairy milk, 3 tablespoons (45 ml) fresh lemon juice, 1 tablespoon (16 g) tahini, 1 tablespoon (15 ml) apple cider vinegar, 1 clove garlic, minced, ½ teaspoon harissa, ¼ teaspoon fine sea salt, and a pinch of white pepper in a blender. Process until smooth. Stir in 1 teaspoon fresh minced chives and adjust the seasonings.

**TO ASSEMBLE THE SANDWICHES:** Fill each pita pocket evenly with 5 of the falafel patties, lettuce, tomatoes, and cucumber and drizzle the sauce over all.

# PORTOBELLO PO' BOYS

Our version of the po' boy echoes the seafood version popular in New Orleans. Imagine: perfectly spiced breaded portobello strips, crisp fresh vegetables, and a tangy sauce, all on a baguette. Better yet, go make it!

**YIELD**
4 SANDWICHES

### FOR SPREAD

½ cup (112 g) vegan mayonnaise

2 tablespoons (20 g) minced onion

1 tablespoon (4 g) minced fresh parsley

2 teaspoons Dijon mustard

2 teaspoons sweet relish

1 teaspoon sriracha, to taste

Salt and pepper, to taste

### FOR MUSHROOMS

3 tablespoons (23 g) all-purpose flour

3 tablespoons (26 g) cornmeal

1½ tablespoons (2 g) Creole seasoning

½ cup plus 2 tablespoons (150 ml) nondairy milk

1 tablespoon (15 g) Dijon mustard

Canola oil, for cooking

4 large portobello mushrooms, stemmed and cut into ½-inch (1.3-cm) slices

### FOR SANDWICHES

One 20-inch (51-cm) baguette, cut in half lengthwise, cut into 4 pieces, and some inside removed

2 cups (140 g) shredded lettuce

2 large tomatoes, sliced

3 thin slices red onion, separated into rings

4 dill pickles, sliced

**TO MAKE THE SEASONING:** In a small bowl, combine all the ingredients. Store in an airtight container.

**TO MAKE THE SPREAD:** In a small bowl, stir together all the ingredients. Refrigerate in an airtight container for up to 1 week.

**TO MAKE THE MUSHROOMS:** Combine the flour, cornmeal, and Creole seasoning in a shallow dish. In a second dish, stir together the milk and mustard. Heat ¼ inch (6 mm) oil in a large skillet over medium heat. Preheat the oven to 250°F (120°C, or gas mark ½). Line a baking sheet with paper towels. With one hand, dip the mushroom slices into the milk mixture, then with the other hand into the flour mixture. Transfer to the skillet and fry until golden, turning once, 4 to 5 minutes. Transfer to the baking sheet to drain and keep warm in the oven.

**TO ASSEMBLE THE SANDWICHES:** Smear 1 tablespoon (17 g) spread on both sides of the bread. Layer the mushrooms, lettuce, tomatoes, red onion, and dill pickles on top. Top with the other slice of bread and serve.

**FOR CREOLE SEASONING:** In a small bowl, combine 1 tablespoon (7 g) paprika, 1 teaspoon garlic powder, 1 teaspoon onion powder, 1 teaspoon dried thyme, 1 teaspoon cayenne pepper, ½ teaspoon fine sea salt, ½ teaspoon black pepper.

# RETRO KFC-STYLE SANDWICHES

Back in 1981, the restaurant version of this sandwich was the very last meat that Tami ever ate. Besides tasting much better than the meaty original, this dish comes together in a flash.

**YIELD**
4 SANDWICHES

## FOR SAUCE

½ cup (112 g) vegan mayonnaise

2 tablespoons (20 g) minced red onion

2 tablespoons (30 g) minced dill pickle

1 teaspoon ume plum vinegar

¼ teaspoon white pepper

## FOR FRIED SEITAN

1½ cups (42 g) cornflakes, crushed into crumbs

Pinch of salt and pepper

1 teaspoon dried parsley

1 teaspoon dried thyme

1 teaspoon onion powder

1 teaspoon fine sea salt

½ teaspoon mustard powder

½ teaspoon paprika

¼ teaspoon cayenne pepper

¼ teaspoon black pepper

¼ cup plus 2 tablespoons (47 g) all-purpose flour

½ cup (120 ml) nondairy milk, plus additional 2 tablespoons (30 ml), if needed

Canola oil, for cooking

4 No Cluck Cutlets (page 181)

## FOR SANDWICHES

4 burger buns, split in half, toasted

3 cups (212 g) finely shredded lettuce

1 large tomato, sliced

**TO MAKE THE SAUCE:** Mix all the ingredients together in a small bowl. Refrigerate in an airtight container.

**TO MAKE THE CUTLETS:** Combine the cornflakes and a pinch of salt and pepper in a pie plate or shallow dish. In a second pie plate, combine the parsley, thyme, onion powder, salt, mustard powder, paprika, cayenne, black pepper, and flour. Mix with a fork. Add ½ cup (120 ml) milk to the flour mixture, adding the remaining milk 1 tablespoon (15 ml) at a time, if needed, to make a smooth batter.

Line a plate with paper towels. Pour enough canola oil into a large skillet to cover the bottom. Heat over medium heat. Dip each cutlet into the batter, then into the cornflakes. Carefully place the cutlets in the hot oil. Cook for 3 to 4 minutes, or until golden. Turn and cook the other side for 2 to 3 minutes, or until golden. Transfer to the plate to drain.

**TO ASSEMBLE THE SANDWICHES:** Spread the sauce evenly on the inside of the buns. Place a cutlet on each bun and top with ¾ cup (53 g) of the lettuce, a tomato slice, and the bun tops. Serve.

### SERVING SUGGESTIONS AND VARIATIONS

• If you prefer, this may be made with 1 pound (454 g) extra-firm tofu, drained and pressed. Cut the tofu into 4 slabs. Brush with 2 tablespoons (30 ml) tamari. Reduce the batter and cornflake amounts by half. Otherwise, proceed as above.

• These make wonderful picnic sandwiches. Package the sauce (keep it cool), seitan/tofu, vegetables, and buns separately.

• The cutlets (either seitan or tofu) are delicious served "homestyle" with mashed potatoes and gravy.

# DAGWOOD'S SPECIAL SANDWICH

This iconic American sandwich was inspired by the Blondie comic strip, which was first published in 1930. Dagwood, one of the main characters, was notorious for raiding the refrigerator to create mile-high stacked sandwiches. In our little corner of the world, we like to think that Dagwood just went vegan. You will need two long bamboo skewers, cut in half, to keep the stacks together and get the full effect.

**YIELD**
4 SANDWICHES

**FOR SPREAD**

⅓ cup (75 g) vegan mayonnaise

2 tablespoons (30 g) yellow mustard

¼ teaspoon cayenne pepper (optional)

**FOR SANDWICHES**

6 slices sandwich bread, toasted

1 head romaine lettuce, torn into sandwich-size leaves

4 ounces (113 g) thin Mushroom Tomato Slices (pages 183)

4 ounces (113 g) thin Gobbler Slices (page 182)

8 ounces (227 g) tempeh bacon, homemade (page 179) or store-bought, cooked

1 green bell pepper, cored and cut into rings

1 large tomato, sliced

3 thin slices red onion, cut into half-moons, separated

20 dill pickle slices

4 olives or small pickles, for garnish

**TO MAKE THE SPREAD:** Mix all the ingredients together in a small bowl. Store in an airtight container in the refrigerator until ready to use.

**TO ASSEMBLE THE SANDWICHES:** Smear a generous 1 table-spoon (18 g) spread on each slice of bread. Divide the lettuce leaves evenly on 4 of the slices. Divide the Mushroom Tomato Slices, Gobbler Slices, and tempeh bacon evenly among the sandwiches. Top with the bell pepper, tomato, onion, and dill pickle slices. Put one topless stack on each one of the others. Top each stack with the 2 remaining slices of bread. Place 2 skewers through each sandwich and put an olive or a pickle on the skewer. Cut the sandwiches in half and serve.

**RECIPE NOTE**

If you prefer to use store-bought tempeh bacon, go ahead and just use the 6-ounce (170-g) package.

# PÂTÉ SANDWICHES

Have your *béret* and fake *moustache* handy. We're going French here by rocking rich pâté on some crusty baguette while listening to our favorite Edith Piaf songs.

**YIELD**
8 SANDWICHES
2 CUPS (230 G) PARMESAN
2 ¼ CUPS (680 G) PÂTÉ

**FOR VEGAN PARMESAN**

1 cup (128 g) whole, dry-roasted, lightly salted cashews

1 clove garlic, minced

1 tablespoon (15 g) maca powder (optional)

½ cup (60 g) nutritional yeast

¼ cup (28 g) coconut flour or (20 g) bread crumbs, or a combination of the two

1 tablespoon (7 g) white miso

**FOR PÂTÉ**

1 tablespoon (15 ml) olive oil

8 ounces (227 g) cremini mushrooms, sliced

¾ cup (120 g) chopped red onion

4 cloves garlic, pressed

Salt and pepper, to taste

1 teaspoon Italian seasoning

1 tablespoon (15 ml) fresh lemon juice

¼ cup (64 g) toasted creamy cashew or almond butter

½ cup (58 g) Vegan Parmesan

1 cup (240 g) cooked chickpeas or (262 g) cannellini beans

**FOR SANDWICHES**

16 baguette slices, ½ inch (1.3 cm) thick, lightly toasted if desired

1 cup (40 g) packed fresh herb salad mix or 16 endive leaves

1 crisp pear, quartered, cored, and each quarter thinly sliced

**TO MAKE THE PARMESAN:** Combine all the ingredients in a food processor and process until crumbly, like Parmesan. Store in an airtight container in the fridge for up to 2 weeks.

**TO MAKE THE PÂTÉ:** Heat the oil in a large skillet. Add the mushrooms, onion, garlic, salt and pepper, and seasoning. Cook over medium-high heat until the mushrooms render their moisture and the onion is tender, about 6 minutes, stirring occasionally.

Add the mushroom mixture to the food processor along with the lemon juice, cashew butter, Vegan Parmesan, and chickpeas. Process until smooth, stopping occasionally to scrape the sides of the food processor with a rubber spatula. Continue processing just a little more, until fluffy and airy. Use at room temperature or chilled. Store in an airtight container in the fridge for up to 1 week.

**TO ASSEMBLE THE SANDWICHES:** Spread 1 tablespoon (17 g) pâté (or enough to cover the whole surface) on each slice of baguette. Top with just enough salad or 2 endive leaves to cover 8 of the slices, adding 2 thin slices of pear on top of the salad. Crack some extra pepper over the pear if desired, and top with the other slice of baguette.

**SERVING SUGGESTIONS AND VARIATIONS**

• You can use the extra Parmesan anywhere Vegan Parmesan is called for, such as in our recipe for Croque-Monsieur (page 119).

• There will be leftover pâté as well, which makes for a perfect snack or appetizer when served on seedy crackers.

# PITTSBURGH STEAK SANDWICHES

Philadelphia made its mark on sandwiches with its namesake cheesesteak. We think you'll agree that this cheese-free sandwich more than rivals the Philly. Once the seitan is in the oven, this practically jumps onto the table, leaving the cow another day to jump over the moon.

**YIELD**
4 SANDWICHES

½ cup (120 ml) vegetable broth

¼ cup (60 ml) vegan red wine

1 tablespoon (15 ml) balsamic vinegar

1 tablespoon (15 ml) tamari

½ teaspoon vegan Worcestershire sauce

¼ teaspoon fine sea salt

½ teaspoon black pepper

1 pound (454 g) Moo-Free Seitan (page 180), cut into ⅛-inch (3-mm) slices

⅓ cup (75 g) vegan mayonnaise

2 cloves garlic, minced

Pepper, to taste

4 ciabatta rolls, sliced in half

16 lettuce leaves

2 tomatoes, cut into ½-inch (1.3-cm) slices

1 avocado, pitted, peeled, and sliced

Preheat the oven to 400°F (200°C, or gas mark 6). In a 9 x 13-inch (23 x 33-cm) pan, combine the broth, wine, vinegar, tamari, Worcestershire sauce, salt, and pepper. Put the seitan slices into the pan and turn to coat. Bake for 30 to 35 minutes, or until most of the marinade has been absorbed.

Combine the mayonnaise, garlic, and a pinch of pepper in a small bowl. Spread the sauce on the inside tops of the rolls. Place the lettuce on the bottom. Divide the seitan, tomato slices, and avocado slices on top of the seitan. Put on the top of the bun and serve.

### SERVING SUGGESTIONS AND VARIATIONS

• These might be messy for the road, but if you're eating at a picnic table, they're just as great at room temperature as they are hot. Pack the seitan and vegetables in separate containers. Keep the mayo cool, and pile them together when ready.

• For a Philly-style seitan sandwich, omit the avocado. Sprinkle nondairy cheese on each sliced ciabatta and broil for 2 to 3 minutes until melted. Proceed as above.

# FROM RUSSIA WITH LOVE

These flavors blend together in perfect harmony, just like back in the U.S.S.R.

| YIELD |
|---|
| 8 SANDWICHES |

## FOR TEMPEH

1½ cups (355 ml) vegetable broth

2 small pickled beets

⅓ cup (50 g) minced shallot

1 tablespoon plus 1 teaspoon (20 ml) tamari

1 tablespoon plus 1 teaspoon (20 ml) apple cider vinegar

1 tablespoon (15 ml) liquid smoke

1 teaspoon agave nectar

½ teaspoon fine sea salt

½ teaspoon black pepper

2 packages (8 ounces, or 227 g each) tempeh

1 tablespoon (15 ml) canola oil

## FOR SPREAD AND SANDWICHES

¼ cup plus 2 tablespoons (80 g) nondairy sour cream

¼ cup (60 ml) dill pickle juice

1 tablespoon plus 1 teaspoon (20 g) prepared horseradish

2 teaspoons Dijon mustard

1 teaspoon dried dillweed

1 teaspoon agave nectar

½ teaspoon black pepper

¼ cup (40 g) minced onion

¼ cup (60 g) minced dill pickle

2 cups (284 g) sauerkraut, drained

1 teaspoon caraway seeds

½ teaspoon smoked paprika

½ teaspoon black pepper

¼ cup (56 g) nondairy butter

16 slices pumpernickel or rye bread, 4 inches (10 cm) wide

**TO MAKE THE TEMPEH:** Cut the tempeh in half lenghtwise, then across to make 8 patties. Combine the broth, beets, shallot, tamari, vinegar, liquid smoke, agave, salt, and black pepper in a blender. Blend until smooth. Pour into a 9 x 13-inch (23 x 33-cm) pan. Add the tempeh patties and turn to coat. Let marinate in the refrigerator for 1 hour or longer.

**TO MAKE THE SPREAD AND SANDWICHES:** In a small bowl, stir all the ingredients together. Refrigerate in an airtight container.

Heat the canola oil in a large skillet over medium-high heat. Drain the tempeh and add it to the pan. Sauté for 5 minutes, or until blackened. Turn over and cook the other side for 4 minutes.

**TO ASSEMBLE THE SANDWICHES:** Combine the sauerkraut, caraway, paprika, and black pepper in a medium-size sauce-pan and warm over medium heat.

Preheat a panini press fitted with smooth plates on high. Butter the bread slices. Smear 1 tablespoon (25 g) spread on the unbuttered sides of 8 slices. Place 1 tempeh patty on each slice. Top with ¼ cup (36 g) sauerkraut. Smear the remaining spread on the remaining 8 slices. Put the tops on, buttered sides out. With the grill open, cook until golden, 4 to 5 minutes. Turn over and cook the other side for 3 to 4 minutes. Cut in half and serve.

### SERVING SUGGESTIONS AND VARIATIONS

For a side dish, we opt for just a few baked potato wedges. If you'd like, make more of the spread to dip the potato wedges into.

# RATATOUILLE SANDWICHES

Here are all the flavors of summer and Provence rolled into one. Don't be too surprised if you start hearing cicadas as you bite into one of these.

**YIELD**
6 SANDWICHES
1½ CUPS (410 G) SPREAD

### FOR SPREAD

1 can (15 ounces, or 425 g) chickpeas, drained and rinsed

¼ cup (35 g) roasted red bell pepper

2 tablespoons (14 g) sliced sun-dried tomatoes in oil, drained

1 tablespoon (8 g) drained capers

1 tablespoon (15 ml) olive oil

2 cloves garlic, pressed

1½ tablespoons (25 ml) fresh lemon juice

¼ to ½ teaspoon red pepper flakes, to taste

Salt and pepper, to taste

### FOR SANDWICHES

2 tablespoons (30 ml) olive oil

2 teaspoons fresh lemon juice

Salt and pepper, to taste

12 half-moon slices eggplant, ¼ inch (6 mm) thick

12 slices zucchini, ¼ inch (6 mm) thick

6 slices red onion, ¼ inch (6 mm) thick

1 loaf Green Monster Bread (page 178), cut into 12 slices, or any crusty bread, toasted, rubbed with garlic clove

6 thin slices beefsteak tomato

6 quarters roasted yellow bell peppers, drained

12 leaves fresh basil, cut into chiffonade

6 tablespoons (23 g) chopped fresh parsley

**TO MAKE THE SPREAD:** Combine all the ingredients in a food processor and blend until smooth, stopping to scrape down the sides once or twice. Place in an airtight container and chill for a couple of hours.

**TO ASSEMBLE THE SANDWICHES:** Combine the olive oil, lemon juice, salt, and pepper in a small bowl. Lightly brush the mixture on the eggplant, zucchini, and onion slices. Heat a grill or grill pan over medium-high heat and grill the vegetables until they are just tender and have grill marks, about 4 minutes on each side.

Smear 1 tablespoon (17 g) of the spread on all the slices of toasted bread. Place 2 slices eggplant, 2 slices zucchini, 1 slice tomato, 1 slice onion, separated into rings so that there's onion in every bite; 1 quarter roasted pepper, 2 leaves basil, and 1 tablespoon (4 g) parsley on top. Season with extra salt and pepper, if desired. Top with the second slice of bread. Serve immediately.

# WINGWICH

Hot wings are hugely popular in the United States, and the heat factor ranges from mild to fiery. We prefer Frank's brand, the traditional hot sauce. Our version is more flavorful than all-out hot, and it's accented by the slaw. Don't mention the coffee, and see if anyone can guess the subtle undertone.

**YIELD**
4 SANDWICHES

4 cups (280 g) shredded green cabbage

1 cup (70 g) shredded red cabbage

¼ cup (56 g) vegan mayonnaise, to taste

1 teaspoon apple cider vinegar

½ teaspoon celery salt

Pinch of black pepper

2 teaspoons nondairy butter

½ cup (120 ml) hot sauce

2 tablespoons (30 ml) brewed coffee

1 to 2 tablespoons (15 to 30 ml) canola oil, divided

1 pound (454 g) Moo-Free Seitan (page 180) (see Note)

4 thick slices ciabatta bread

1 medium-size cucumber, sliced into rounds

2 slices red onion, separated

In a medium-size bowl, combine the cabbages, mayonnaise, vinegar, celery salt, and black pepper. Stir to combine. Store in an airtight container in the refrigerator until ready to use.

In a small saucepan over medium heat, melt the butter. Add the hot sauce and coffee. Stir to combine.

Heat a large skillet over medium-high heat. Add 1 tablespoon (15 ml) of the oil and the seitan. Stir and cook until browned, 8 to 10 minutes. Add the remaining 1 tablespoon (15 ml) oil while cooking if the seitan is sticking. Remove from the heat. Pour the sauce into the skillet and stir to coat the seitan.

To assemble the sandwiches, place a slice of ciabatta on each plate. Divide the slaw, cucumber, and onion evenly among the slices. Divide the seitan among the sandwiches and serve.

**RECIPE NOTE**

While the seitan is still warm, cut off a 1-pound (454-g) portion. Using two forks, pull it apart to create bite-size pieces to use as wings. Refrigerate in an airtight container until ready to use. The seitan should be cooled before cooking. As with all seitan, the wings freeze well.

**SERVING SUGGESTIONS AND VARIATIONS**

• This can also be made with 1 pound (454 g) extra-firm tofu, drained, pressed, and cut into 1-inch (2.5-cm) cubes. Proceed as above.

• Yes, you're right (and so were our testers): this sandwich cries out for celery sticks. Rather than add them to the sandwich, we suggest serving them on the side.

# UNFISHWICH

Nothing fishy going on here! Kelp, a seaweed that is packed with vitamins and minerals, does a great job mimicking the flavor of the fish sticks of our childhood, in its own cruelty-free way.

**YIELD**
3 SANDWICHES

### FOR TARTAR SAUCE

½ cup (120 g) miso dressing (page 107)

1 to 2 teaspoons fresh lemon juice, to taste

½ teaspoon minced capers

1 teaspoon Dijon mustard

1 teaspoon minced shallot

Few drops hot sauce

### FOR FISH STICKS

8 ounces (227 g) tempeh

2 tablespoons plus 2 teaspoons (40 ml) fresh lemon juice, divided

⅓ cup plus ¼ cup (140 ml) unsweetened plain nondairy milk, divided

1 teaspoon kelp powder

1 teaspoon onion powder

2 cloves garlic, pressed

1 teaspoon paprika

½ teaspoon fine sea salt, plus a pinch

½ teaspoon dried dillweed

⅓ cup (42 g) arrowroot powder

1 tablespoon (2 g) Old Bay seasoning, divided

¾ cup (60 g) bread crumbs

Nonstick cooking spray

3 tablespoons (42 g) nondairy butter, melted

¼ teaspoon cayenne pepper, to taste

### FOR SANDWICHES

3 sub sandwich rolls, 6 inches (15 cm) long

¾ cup (78 g) thinly sliced cucumber

2 small tomatoes, thinly sliced

**TO MAKE THE TARTAR SAUCE:** Combine all the ingredients in a medium-size bowl. Store in an airtight container in the fridge until ready to use.

**TO MAKE THE FISH STICKS:** Cut the tempeh widthwise into 9 sticks. Combine 2 tablespoons (30 ml) lemon juice, ⅓ cup (80 ml) milk, kelp powder, onion powder, garlic, paprika, ½ teaspoon salt, and dillweed in a shallow dish. Add the tempeh sticks and let marinate for 1 hour in the fridge.

Line a baking sheet with parchment paper or a silicone baking mat. Preheat the oven to 375°F (190°C, or gas mark 5).

Combine the arrowroot powder with 2 teaspoons Old Bay seasoning in a shallow plate; place the bread crumbs in another plate. Remove the sticks from the marinade, and thin out the marinade by adding the remaining ¼ cup (60 ml) milk.

Dip the sticks into the arrowroot, shaking off any excess. Dip the sticks into the marinade, shaking off any excess, and then coat with the bread crumbs. Place on the prepared baking sheet. Lightly coat all sides with cooking spray. Bake for 10 minutes.

Combine the butter, 2 teaspoons lemon juice, cayenne pepper, 1 teaspoon Old Bay seasoning, and a pinch of salt in a small bowl.

**TO ASSEMBLE THE SANDWICHES:** Cut the rolls in half lengthwise and lightly toast them. Spread 2 tablespoons (30 ml) tartar sauce on each side of the roll. Divide the sliced cucumber and tomatoes among the sandwiches, add 3 sticks to each sandwich, and serve immediately.

# CROQUINOETTE WRAP PARTY

These little croquettes get beautifully crusty once you panfry them in sesame oil. Liz Wyman, who is one of our VITPs (as in, very important tester-person), described the combination of all components as being a bit like hummus, but "burgerified."

### YIELD
8 WRAPS, 1 CUP (240 G) DRESSING

### FOR MISO DRESSING

4 ounces (113 g) drained firm silken tofu

3 tablespoons (24 g) white miso

3 tablespoons (45 ml) olive oil

3 tablespoons (45 ml) white balsamic vinegar

½ teaspoon ground black pepper, to taste

Smoked sea salt, to taste

1 clove garlic

### FOR CROQUETTES

1 can (15 ounces, or 425 g) chickpeas, drained and rinsed

2 tablespoons (32 g) creamy natural peanut butter

2 tablespoons (16 g) white miso

2 tablespoons (30 ml) fresh lemon juice

2 tablespoons (15 g) nutritional yeast

2 cloves garlic, pressed

2 cups (370 g) cooked and cooled quinoa

¼ cup (20 g) bread crumbs

2 tablespoons (16 g) cornstarch

1 cup (150 g) grated zucchini

2 tablespoons (20 g) minced shallot

Salt and pepper, to taste

2 tablespoons (30 ml) toasted sesame oil, divided

### FOR WRAPS

1 English cucumber, cut in half lengthwise and cut into thin half-moons

Eight 8-inch (20 cm) flour tortillas

Sriracha, for serving (optional)

**TO MAKE THE DRESSING:** Blend all the ingredients in a blender. Store in an airtight container and chill until ready to serve.

**TO MAKE THE CROQUETTES:** Place the chickpeas, peanut butter, miso, lemon juice, nutritional yeast, and garlic in a food processor. Process until smooth, stopping to scrape the sides of the bowl. Place in a large bowl and add the quinoa, bread crumbs, cornstarch, zucchini, shallot, salt, and pepper. Combine thoroughly without mashing too much. The mixture will look wet. Cover the bowl and chill for 1 hour. Divide into 8 croquettes by scooping out a packed ⅓ cup (105 g) per croquette and shaping into a 3-inch (8-cm)-wide round.

Heat 1 tablespoon (15 ml) of the oil in a large skillet over medium-high heat and cook the croquettes in batches for 6 minutes on each side: the croquette must get a golden-brown, crispy crust. Adjust the heat, if needed, and use the remaining tablespoon (15 ml) of oil if needed as you cook the croquettes.

**TO ASSEMBLE THE WRAPS:** Divide the sliced cucumber evenly among all 8 tortillas, drizzle as much dressing as desired on top, place a croquette on top and fold the tortilla over. Add sriracha, if desired.

### RECIPE NOTES

• If you do not want to eat all the croquettes at once, wrap them well once they are shaped, and they will keep for at least 4 days in the fridge. You can just cook them as you need them.

• The leftover dressing will keep well for about a week, stored in an airtight container, and is also a great dip for crudités and steamed vegetables, or to serve alongside vegan meats and other burgers. It is the base for the spreads in the Razz-elnut Spinach Sandwiches (page 64), Unfishwich (page 104), and Out of Tuna Sandwiches (page 132).

# BEAN AND NUT BURGERS

We're proud to present a burger that's ready in minutes and made of simple ingredients you're almost guaranteed to have at all times in your fridge and pantry. Not to mention the most important part: it really is a treat to eat!

**YIELD**
4 SANDWICHES

1 can (15 ounces, or 425 g) cannellini or black beans, drained and rinsed

¼ cup (30 g) walnut pieces

¼ cup (60 ml) barbecue sauce, homemade (page 123) or store-bought, plus extra for serving if desired

2 tablespoons (14 g) onion powder or ¼ cup (40 g) finely chopped onion

1½ teaspoons garlic powder or 1 tablespoon (8 g) minced garlic

½ teaspoon fine sea salt, to taste

½ teaspoon cayenne pepper

½ teaspoon black pepper, to taste

½ cup (40 g) panko or regular bread crumbs, plus more if needed

Peanut oil, for panfrying

4 burger buns

Onion rings (page 38), tomato slices, or other burger toppings

Place the beans, walnuts, barbecue sauce, onion powder, garlic powder, salt, cayenne, and black pepper in a food processor. Pulse a few times until the beans are slightly mashed but not completely puréed.

Remove half of the mixture and place in a bowl. Add the panko to the remaining half of the mixture in the food processor. Process until mostly smooth.

Combine both halves of the mixture. Add more bread crumbs if the mixture is too wet, and more barbecue sauce if it is too dry. Divide the mixture into 4 equal portions of approximately ½ cup (130 g) each. Shape into burgers about 3 inches (8 cm) wide and ½ inch (1.3 cm) thick.

Lightly grease a skillet with peanut oil, heat over medium heat, add the burgers, and cook for 5 minutes on each side, or until golden brown.

Serve each burger in a bun, with the usual fixings, along with a little extra barbecue sauce.

**SERVING SUGGESTIONS AND VARIATIONS**

Although we're huge fans of sandwiches and mile-high burgers, we occasionally like to eat this one bun-free, with a simple side of salad or steamed veggies when we're really not in the mood for bread. It happens to the best of us.

# GREEK BURGERS

When we think of Greece, we think of blue skies and sunshine, perfect temperatures, white beaches, and all the Mediterranean flavors we packed into these burgers. Top with the usual fixings.

### FOR BURGERS

⅔ cup (160 ml) boiling water

½ cup (50 g) texturized vegetable protein

3 tablespoons (45 g) ketchup

1 teaspoon vegan Worcestershire sauce

1 cup plus 2 tablespoons (162 g) vital wheat gluten

¼ cup (28 g) finely minced sun-dried tomatoes (moist vacuum-packed, not oil-packed)

3 tablespoons (30 g) red onion, finely minced

2 tablespoons (13 g) kalamata olives, finely minced

2 artichoke hearts, finely minced

2 tablespoons (15 g) nutritional yeast

2 teaspoons dried oregano

1 teaspoon ground coriander

1 teaspoon ground cumin

1 teaspoon onion powder

½ teaspoon fine sea salt

½ teaspoon black pepper

1 tablespoon (15 to 30 ml) vegetable broth, if needed

### FOR SPREAD

⅓ cup (75 g) vegan mayonnaise

2 tablespoons (30 ml) fresh lemon juice

2 cloves garlic, minced

### FOR SANDWICHES

Canola oil, for cooking

6 English muffins, toasted

**TO MAKE THE BURGERS:** Combine the water, texturized vegetable protein, ketchup, and Worcestershire in a medium-size bowl and stir. Let sit for 5 minutes. Add the vital wheat gluten, sun-dried tomatoes, onion, olives, artichoke hearts, nutritional yeast, and spices. Mix well and knead until cohesive. If the mixture is dry, add 1 tablespoon (15 ml) vegetable broth.

Prepare a steamer. Divide the mixture evenly among six 10-inch (25-cm) pieces of foil. Form into burgers 3½ to 4 inches (8 to 10 cm) wide, pressing any loose vegetables into the burgers. Fold the foil around the burgers. Steam for 1 hour. Chill before using.

**TO MAKE THE SPREAD:** In a small bowl, mix the mayonnaise, lemon juice, and garlic. Season to taste.

**TO ASSEMBLE THE BURGERS:** Lightly oil a large skillet and heat over medium-high heat. Cook the burgers until nearly blackened on the bottom, about 4 minutes. Turn and cook the other side. Smear 1 tablespoon (14 g) spread on one side of 6 muffins. Put a burger on the muffin and top with the muffin tops.

**SERVING SUGGESTIONS AND VARIATIONS**

We like these with some Greek Potato Wedges on the side.

# BEET-N-BARLEY BURGERS

These delectable burgers hit the mark even with nonbeet lovers. The slightly earthy undertone is the perfect springboard for the black-eyed peas and barley. For a milder burger, use golden beets. Keep in mind that beets stain.

**YIELD**
8 BURGERS

4 cups (940 ml) water

½ cup (100 g) dry pearl barley

Pinch of salt

1 tablespoon (15 ml) olive oil

1 cup (160 g) minced onion

1 cup (225 g) peeled, finely diced raw beets

½ cup (75 g) minced green bell pepper

3 tablespoons (24 g) minced carrot

3 cloves garlic, pressed

1 teaspoon smoked paprika

1 teaspoon ground cumin

1 teaspoon dried thyme

½ cup (86 g) cooked black-eyed peas, drained and rinsed

¼ cup (65 g) barbecue sauce, homemade (page 123) or store-bought

2 teaspoons Dijon mustard

1 teaspoon liquid smoke

1 teaspoon ume plum vinegar

½ teaspoon fine sea salt

¼ teaspoon black pepper

⅔ to 1 cup (60 to 90 g) old-fashioned or quick oats, ground

Canola oil, for cooking

8 burger buns

Vegan mayonnaise, onions, lettuce, tomato, pickles, or other burger toppings

Combine the water, barley, and a pinch of salt in a medium-size saucepan and bring to a boil over high heat. Reduce to a simmer and cook, uncovered, for 30 to 35 minutes, or until the barley is quite tender. Drain.

Heat the oil in a large skillet over medium heat. Add the onion, beets, bell pepper, carrot, garlic, and spices and cook, stirring, until the vegetables are tender, about 10 minutes. Set aside.

In a large bowl, mash the black-eyed peas with a fork until pasty. Add the barbecue sauce, mustard, liquid smoke, vinegar, salt, and pepper. Stir to combine. Add the barley and vegetables. Stir well to combine. Add ⅔ cup (60 g) ground oats and mix well. Add more ground oats, 1 tablespoon (8 g) at a time, until the mixture can be shaped into burgers. At this point, refrigerate the mixture for 1 hour or longer.

Line a baking sheet with parchment paper. Using ½ cup (112 g) of the mixture, form into 8 patties about 3 inches (8 cm) wide and ½ inch (1.3 cm) thick.

Heat enough canola oil to cover the bottom of a large skillet over medium-high heat. Add the burgers and cook for 5 to 6 minutes, or until the bottom is blackened and slightly crisp. Turn over and cook the other side for 4 to 5 minutes. Serve on the buns with desired toppings.

**SERVING SUGGESTIONS AND VARIATIONS**

Call us traditional, but we usually serve these with mayo, lettuce, and a tomato slice. But we've been known to try them topped with salsa and some smashed avocado on the bun. For a Southern feel, we also love them with corn salsa and red onion. Mango chutney and alfalfa sprouts give the burgers a whole different twist.

# MEAT(LESS)BALL SUBS

Since we didn't grow up eating meatball subs, we were surprised by how popular they are. These became a nostalgic favorite among testers and their husbands who had been searching for a just-right meatless ball. With gentle handling, you'll have minimal crumbling.

**YIELD**
4 SUBS

## FOR MEATLESS BALLS

⅔ cup (160 ml) boiling water

¾ cup (75 g) texturized vegetable protein

½ cup (80 g) minced onion

3 cloves garlic, minced

1½ teaspoons Italian seasoning blend

½ teaspoon dried parsley

¼ teaspoon red pepper flakes, to taste

2 tablespoons (33 g) tomato paste

1 teaspoon vegan Worcestershire sauce

1 cup (144 g) vital wheat gluten, or more if needed

2 tablespoons (30 ml) olive oil

1 cup (235 ml) vegetable broth

¼ cup (60 ml) dry red wine (optional)

## FOR SANDWICHES

2 tablespoons (30 ml) olive oil, divided

1 medium-size onion, cut into thin half-moons

1 green bell pepper, cored and cut into strips

4 sub rolls, wedges cut out of tops, some of the bread removed, and toasted

1⅓ cups (333 g) favorite marinara, warmed

**TO MAKE THE MEATLESS BALLS:** In a small bowl, combine the water and texturized vegetable protein. Place the onion, garlic, seasoning blend, parsley, red pepper flakes, tomato paste, and Worcestershire sauce in a food processor and pulse until combined. Add the texturized vegetable protein, any unabsorbed water, and the vital wheat gluten. Pulse until thoroughly combined and the mixture can be formed into balls. If it is too sticky, add 1 tablespoon (9 g) vital wheat gluten and mix again. Roll about a rounded tablespoon (30 g) of the mixture into a tightly compressed ball. Repeat to form 16 to 20 balls.

Preheat the oven to 300°F (150°C, or gas mark 2). Heat the oil in a large oven-safe skillet over medium-high heat. Brown the balls, about 5 minutes. Turn gently to brown all sides. Remove from the heat. Add the broth and wine to the skillet and cover tightly with foil. Bake for 20 minutes. Remove from the oven and carefully turn the balls over. Recover tightly with foil and bake for 20 more minutes. Remove the foil and bake uncovered for 10 minutes, or until the liquid has been absorbed. Chill before using.

**TO ASSEMBLE THE SANDWICHES:** Heat 1 tablespoon (15 ml) of the oil in a large skillet over medium heat. Add the onion and cook for 2 minutes. Add the bell pepper and cook for 3 minutes; the vegetables should remain crisp. Transfer to a plate. Add the remaining oil and the balls. Cook, turning gently, for 5 minutes, or until heated through. Divide the vegetables evenly among the rolls and add 4 or 5 balls each. Top each with ⅓ cup (83 g) marinara. Serve.

# PEANUT BUTTER BANANA BACON SANDWICHES

Oh yes, we did. If you're in a pinch and prefer using panfried and ready-to-go tempeh bacon (page 179) instead of the "fiberful" chickpea goodness here, it will work well, too.

| YIELD |
|---|
| 4 SANDWICHES |

**FOR CHICKPEA BACON**

1 can (15 ounces, or 425 g) chickpeas, drained and rinsed

1 tablespoon (15 ml) pure maple syrup

1½ teaspoons apple cider vinegar

Heaping ¼ teaspoon smoked paprika

½ teaspoon smoked sea salt, to taste

½ teaspoon onion powder

¼ teaspoon garlic powder

2 teaspoons to 1 tablespoon (10 to 15 ml) liquid smoke, to taste

1 tablespoon (15 ml) olive oil

**FOR SANDWICHES**

½ cup (128 g) crunchy, unsweetened natural peanut butter

4 soft bread rolls, cut in half, or 8 slices any bread

2 small, just-ripe bananas, sliced

Nonstick cooking spray or nondairy butter

**TO MAKE THE CHICKPEA BACON:** Preheat the broiler. Combine all the ingredients in a medium-size bowl and then spread in a shallow, 8-inch (20-cm) baking dish. Make sure the chickpeas are in a single layer so they cook evenly. Broil for 8 minutes, stir, and broil for 6 to 8 minutes longer, checking every 2 minutes to make sure the chickpeas don't burn. They are ready when the liquid has been absorbed and the chickpeas are crispy and dark golden brown.

**TO ASSEMBLE THE SANDWICHES:** Spread 1 tablespoon (16 g) peanut butter (or enough to cover the whole surface of the bread) on each slice of bread. Gently press down a generous ⅓ cup (90 g) chickpea bacon (or as much as will fit) into the peanut butter on 4 of the slices. Place as many slices of banana as will fit on top. Put the second peanut-buttered slice on top.

Lightly coat a large skillet with spray, or melt some butter in the skillet. Cook the sandwiches in batches on medium-low heat until golden brown and crispy, about 5 minutes on each side.

These are also great prepared in a closed panini press, for about 6 minutes in all. This will meld the ingredients together a little more than just grilling the sandwich does.

**SERVING SUGGESTIONS AND VARIATIONS**

You might want to consider making a double or triple batch of chickpea bacon to eat as is, because it makes for a delicious snack that will fly out of the bowl faster than you can swat at the hands attempting to steal your beans. If you do make a larger batch, be sure to use a larger baking tray so the chickpeas can be spread in an even layer, not sitting on top of each other, so they all get a chance to brown up.

# DOUBLE-DECKER DELUXE

With three slices of bread, the filling stays hot while the vegetables stay cool. It's the best of both worlds! Marinate the seitan ahead of time, and you can have dinner on the table in minutes.

---

**YIELD**
4 SANDWICHES

### FOR SAUCE

¼ cup (34 g) cashews, soaked in water for 1 hour, then rinsed and drained

3 tablespoons (45 ml) vegetable broth

1 tablespoon (15 ml) red wine vinegar

1 tablespoon (15 ml) fresh lemon juice

1 tablespoon (10 g) minced shallot

1 teaspoon harissa, to taste

¼ teaspoon agave nectar

Generous pinch of black pepper

2 teaspoons minced fresh parsley

### FOR SEITAN

¼ cup (60 ml) vegetable broth

3 tablespoons (45 ml) brewed coffee

1 clove garlic, minced

¼ teaspoon fine sea salt

12 ounces (340 g) Moo-Free Seitan (page 180), thinly sliced

2 teaspoons olive oil

### FOR SANDWICHES

¼ cup (56 g) nondairy butter, softened

12 slices sandwich bread

2 tablespoons (18 g) minced pepperoncinis, patted dry

1 green bell pepper, cored and cut into strips

2 thin slices red onion, cut into half-moons, rings separated

2 teaspoons Dijon mustard

Lettuce leaves

1 tomato, thinly sliced

2 dill pickles, thinly sliced and patted dry

**TO MAKE THE SAUCE:** Combine the cashews, broth, vinegar, lemon juice, shallot, harissa, agave, and black pepper in a blender. Blend until smooth. Stir in the parsley. Refrigerate in an airtight container until ready to use.

**TO MAKE THE SEITAN:** Combine the broth, coffee, garlic, and salt, in an 8 x 12-inch (20 x 30-cm) pan. Add the seitan and toss to coat. Let marinate in the refrigerator for 1 hour or longer.

Heat the oil in a large skillet over medium heat. Drain the seitan, reserving the marinade, and add to the skillet. Cook until lightly browned, about 5 minutes, scraping up any stuck bits. Add the marinade and cook for 5 minutes, or until the liquid has been absorbed.

**TO ASSEMBLE THE SANDWICHES:** Preheat a panini press on high. Butter one side of all the bread slices. Grill 4 slices of bread in the closed press until golden, 4 minutes. Transfer to a cooling rack (this will be for the cold portion). On the unbuttered side of each of 4 other slices, spread 1 table-spoon (15 ml) sauce. Divide the seitan evenly among them, topping with pepperoncinis, bell pepper, and onion. Spread the remaining sauce evenly on the unbuttered side of the 4 remaining slices. Place the sandwiches buttered sides out on the panini press. Close and grill until golden, 4 minutes. To prepare the cold layer, spread mustard on the unbuttered sides of the first grilled bread. Layer with lettuce, tomato, and pickles. When the grilled layer is done, carefully remove from the press and place on top of the cold layer. Turn the sandwich over, so the cold part is on the top, slice, and serve.

# SOMETHING BLACKENED THIS WAY COMES

Author Ray Bradbury imagined a lot of things, but we'll bet this sandwich wasn't one of them. Fresh tomato-cucumber relish is a flavorful foil for the cutlets. This one is wicked good *(pictured on page 8)*.

**YIELD**
4 SANDWICHES

### FOR SPICY CUTLETS

2 teaspoons smoked paprika

2 teaspoons onion powder

1 teaspoon garlic powder

1 teaspoon ground cumin

1 teaspoon dried thyme

½ teaspoon cayenne pepper

½ teaspoon black pepper

½ teaspoon fine sea salt

2 teaspoons olive oil, divided

4 No Cluck Cutlets (page 181)

### FOR TOMATO RELISH

1 cup (180 g) chopped green tomato
(or, if unavailable, red)

1 cup (135 g) diced cucumber

⅔ cup (60 g) minced scallion

2 tablespoons (30 ml) seasoned rice vinegar

1 tablespoon (2.5 g) minced fresh thyme

Salt and pepper, to taste

### FOR SPREAD

½ cup (112 g) vegan mayonnaise

2 teaspoons Dijon mustard, to taste

2 teaspoons sriracha, to taste

### FOR SANDWICHES

Canola oil, for cooking

4 ciabatta rolls, cut in half and toasted

**TO MAKE THE SPICY CUTLETS:** Mix all the spices together on a large plate. Rub ½ teaspoon olive oil onto each cutlet, dividing it between both sides. Press both sides of a cutlet into the spice mixture and set aside. Repeat to coat the remaining cutlets.

**TO MAKE THE RELISH:** Stir all the ingredients together in a medium-size bowl.

**TO MAKE THE SPREAD:** Stir all the ingredients together in a small bowl. Refrigerate in an airtight container until ready to use.

**TO ASSEMBLE THE SANDWICHES:** Lightly oil a large skillet and heat over medium-high heat. Add the cutlets and cook on one side until blackened and the coating adheres, about 4 minutes. Turn and cook the other side for about 3 minutes. Smear the spread evenly on the rolls. Place a cutlet on each roll and top with ½ cup (57 g) relish and the top of the roll. Serve.

**RECIPE NOTES:**

• With all the parts packed separately, this one can definitely go on the road with you.

• Make double the spice mixture, and you'll have dinner on the table even faster next time. The spices are also a great addition to a terrific tofu scramble.

# CROQUE-MONSIEUR

Literally, and courtesy of the French, behold the "Crunch-Mister," which does admittedly sound a little less dreamy when you put it that way. No one seems to know the story behind the origin of this ham and cheese sandwich, but all that matters in the end is that this vegan version is *formidable*. (That's French for "terrific.")

**YIELD**
4 SANDWICHES

### FOR BÉCHAMEL

2 tablespoons (28 g) nondairy butter

2 tablespoons (15 g) all-purpose flour

¾ cup (180 ml) unsweetened plain nondairy milk

¾ cup (180 ml) unsweetened plain nondairy creamer

½ teaspoon fine sea salt, to taste

¼ teaspoon ground black pepper, to taste

⅛ teaspoon grated nutmeg

1¼ cups (94 g) grated cheese (page 51), divided

¼ cup (29 g) Vegan Parmesan (page 98)

### FOR SANDWICHES

8 teaspoons Dijon mustard

8 slices slightly stale, crusty bread

32 thin Mushroom Tomato Slices (page 183)

8 teaspoons nondairy butter plus 1 to 2 tablespoons (14 to 28 g) for the skillet

**TO MAKE THE BÉCHAMEL:** Melt the butter in a small saucepan over medium-low heat. Add the flour and stir until smooth, cooking for about 2 minutes. Slowly add the milk and creamer (beware of potential splatter), whisking continuously, and cook until thickened, about 4 minutes; the sauce should coat the back of a spoon. Remove from the heat. Add the salt, pepper, nutmeg, ¼ cup (19 g) of the grated cheese, and the Vegan Parmesan.

**TO ASSEMBLE THE SANDWICHES:** Spread 2 teaspoons mustard on 4 slices of bread. Place 8 Mushroom Tomato Slices on each slice, and top with ¼ cup (19 g) of the remaining grated cheese. Spread 2 teaspoons butter on each of the 4 remaining slices of bread, and place on top of the cheese.

Melt 1 tablespoon (14 g) of the butter in a large skillet over medium-low heat. Cook the croque-monsieur in batches just until the cheese starts to melt inside, about 4 minutes on each side, flipping once halfway through. Add the remaining 1 tablespoon (14 g) butter to cook the remaining sandwiches, if needed.

Preheat the oven to 450°F (230°C, or gas mark 8). Spread the béchamel on top of the sandwiches. Place the sandwiches on a broiling pan. Broil for 5 minutes, or until the béchamel is lightly browned. Check occasionally to prevent burning. Remove from the oven and serve immediately.

# CHAPTER SIX

## BOLD NEW GROUND

{ **PUSHING THE BOUNDARIES OF TASTE-BUD ADVENTURE. NO PASSPORT REQUIRED!** }

We hinted at international flair in the last chapter, but here's where we get serious about it. After scanning the globe for sandwich specialties, we've put together this selection. We wanted to include a map so you could chart your journey, but it seemed like a bit much. Happy travels!

# MUFFALETTA

Meant to be shared, this New Orleans classic originated in the Italian section of the city. The tangy giardiniera is beautiful atop the cold cuts, making it an eye-pleasing easy make-ahead (and tasty!) sandwich for get-togethers.

**YIELD**
4 TO 6 SERVINGS

### FOR FAST AND FRESH GIARDINIERA

½ cup (50 g) diced cauliflower

¼ cup (35 g) diced zucchini

1½ tablespoons (12 g) diced carrot

1½ tablespoons (11 g) diced celery

1 hot pepper, minced

3 banana pepper rings, minced

¼ cup (25 g) minced black olives

¼ cup (25 g) minced pimento-stuffed green olives

Pinch of dried oregano

Pinch of red pepper flakes

Pinch of black pepper

1½ tablespoons (23 ml) white wine vinegar

1 teaspoon ume plum vinegar

1 teaspoon extra-virgin olive oil

½ teaspoon agave nectar (optional)

### FOR SANDWICHES

1 cup (20 g) baby arugula

One 10-inch (25-cm) round loaf, cut in half laterally, some of the inside removed to hold the filling

4 ounces (113 g) Mushroom Tomato Slices (page 183)

4 ounces (113 g) Gobbler Slices (page 182)

1 roasted red bell pepper, cored and cut into strips

1 large tomato, sliced

**TO MAKE THE GIARDINIERA:** Combine all the vegetables in a medium-size bowl. In a small bowl, whisk together the oregano, red pepper flakes, pepper, vinegars, oil, and agave. Pour over the vegetables and toss to coat. Refrigerate for at least 1 hour before using.

**TO ASSEMBLE THE SANDWICHES:** Layer the arugula on the bottom of the bread. Layer the Mushroom Tomato and Gobbler Slices evenly over the arugula and top with the pepper strips and tomato slices. Carefully top with the giardiniera. Spoon the dressing from the giardiniera on top to taste. Press the top of the loaf on and cut into 4 or 6 wedges for serving.

### SERVING SUGGESTIONS AND VARIATIONS

• Feel free to double the giardiniera to make sandwiches (or a salad) for another day. Just add a can of drained and rinsed white beans and fill a pita pocket with the mixture.

• When packing for a picnic, divide the arugula between the top and bottom of the bread to keep the giardiniera juices from soaking the bread too much.

# THE MAC-SHROOM

Barbecue and mac and cheeze: two quintessential comfort foods buddied up on a bun. Be sure to serve this with a fork—you'll need it. In our testing, kids especially loved these. Thankfully, we all have some kid left in us.

**YIELD**
4 SANDWICHES

### FOR BARBECUE SAUCE

1 teaspoon olive oil

⅓ cup (55 g) finely minced onion

3 cloves garlic, minced

⅓ cup (80 ml) vegetable broth

1 can (6 ounces, or 170 g) tomato paste

¼ cup (60 ml) brewed coffee

¼ cup (80 g) apple butter

3 tablespoons (45 ml) apple cider vinegar

1 tablespoon (15 ml) tamari

1 tablespoon (15 ml) pure maple syrup

2 teaspoons liquid smoke

### FOR MAC AND CHEEZE

¼ cup (60 ml) nondairy milk, plus more if needed

¼ cup (30 g) nutritional yeast

2 teaspoons olive oil

½ teaspoon white miso

¼ teaspoon onion powder

Pinch of garlic powder

Salt and pepper, to taste

1 cup (105 g) dry elbow macaroni, cooked according to package directions, and drained

### FOR SANDWICHES

1 tablespoon (15 ml) canola oil

4 large portobello caps, stemmed and gilled

Salt and pepper, to taste

¼ cup (56 g) vegan mayonnaise (optional)

4 burger buns, toasted

**TO MAKE THE SAUCE:** Heat the oil in a medium-size saucepan over medium heat. Add the onion and garlic and cook for 4 minutes, or until fragrant. Add the remaining ingredients and stir to combine. Simmer, stirring occasionally, for 20 minutes, or until thickened.

**TO MAKE THE MAC AND CHEEZE:** Combine the milk, nutritional yeast, oil, miso, onion powder, garlic powder, salt, and pepper in a medium-size bowl. Whisk until smooth. Add to the cooked macaroni in the saucepan and stir to coat. Heat the mixture over medium-low heat. If the mixture is too dry, add a splash of milk. Taste and adjust the seasonings.

**TO ASSEMBLE THE SANDWICHES:** Heat the oil in a large skillet over medium-high heat. Put the mushrooms in the skillet, caps down. Season with salt and pepper. Cook for 5 minutes, or until browned on one side. Turn and cook the other side for 4 minutes, or until the center is tender. Reduce the heat to low and coat both sides of the mushrooms with the barbecue sauce. Let cook for 4 minutes.

Spread 1 tablespoon (14 g) mayonnaise on the bottom of each bun. Put a mushroom on each bun, cap side down. Spoon ½ cup (80 g) macaroni into each cap. Replace the top of the bun and serve.

### RECIPE NOTES

• To get the best flavor, use the most natural, unsweetened apple butter you can find.

• The sauce can be used as you would any barbecue sauce. Try it on tofu, tempeh, or seitan.

• If you happen to have barbecue sauce left over, it can be frozen for up to 2 months.

# THE PARTY MONSTER

This stuffed loaf is a show-stopper. It can be served hot or at room temperature. Couple it with your favorite marinara sauce for dipping, if desired.

**YIELD**
6 SERVINGS

1 tablespoon (15 ml) olive oil

1 cup (160 g) chopped onion

2 cups (140 g) sliced mushrooms

¼ teaspoon dried oregano

¼ teaspoon dried thyme

Salt and pepper, to taste

1 recipe Green Monster dough (page 178) or favorite bread dough

6 ounces (170 g) thin Mushroom Tomato Slices (page 183)

6 ounces (170 g) thin Gobbler Slices (page 182)

16 mild banana pepper rings

Nonstick cooking spray

Heat the oil in a large skillet over medium-high heat. Add the onion and cook for 2 minutes, then add the mushrooms, oregano, and thyme. Cook for 5 minutes longer, or until the vegetables are softened. Season to taste with salt and pepper. Let cool before using.

After the dough has risen, dump it onto a lightly floured work surface. With a rolling pin, roll into a 12 x 16-inch (30 x 40-cm) rectangle. With the short side across, on the center 6 inches (15 cm), layer half the Mushroom Tomato and Gobbler Slices, all of the onion/mushroom mixture, the remaining Mushroom Tomato and Gobbler Slices, and the pepper rings. Leave a 1-inch (2.5 cm) strip of dough at the top and bottom without filling.

Using a knife, make 6 to 8 cuts on each side of the filling, perpendicular to the filling. Make an equal number of cuts on each side. This is the part that will be braided. Starting at the top, fold an empty strip of dough over the end of the filling. Alternating sides, pull one strip from each side across the filling. Continue until you reach the last strips on each side. Fold the bottom in, then finish the braid. Pat with your hands to help seal the braided strips closed.

Spray a baking sheet with nonstick spray and carefully transfer the dough to the sheet. Let rise, covered with a towel, for 30 minutes, or until nicely puffed.

Preheat the oven to 350°F (180°C, or gas mark 4). Transfer the baking sheet to the oven and bake for 30 to 35 minutes, or until the bottom is browned. Transfer to a rack and let cool for a few minutes before cutting. Cut into six 2-inch (5-cm) strips and serve.

### SERVING SUGGESTIONS AND VARIATIONS

We love homemade breads, but if you just don't have the time, some grocery stores (or pizza places) sell freshly made pizza dough. It works well here.

# TWO TOMATO TANGO

Tangy, fried green tomatoes burst with flavor when combined with our zesty dressing. We love this one with corn on the cob and coleslaw on the side.

**YIELD**
4 SANDWICHES

## FOR DRESSING

½ cup (112 g) vegan mayonnaise

¼ cup (45 g) chopped roasted red bell pepper

2 cloves garlic, minced

1 tablespoon (15 g) prepared horseradish

2 teaspoons fresh lemon juice

2 teaspoons nutritional yeast

1 teaspoon vegan Worcestershire sauce

1 teaspoon sriracha, to taste

1 teaspoon Dijon mustard

Salt and pepper, to taste

¼ cup plus 2 tablespoons (36 g) minced scallion

## FOR FRIED GREEN TOMATOES

½ cup (120 ml) unsweetened plain soymilk

2 teaspoons apple cider vinegar

1 teaspoon prepared horseradish

½ teaspoon fine sea salt

Pinch of black pepper

½ cup (25 g) panko crumbs

1 tablespoon (9 g) cornmeal

1 teaspoon onion powder

Canola oil, for cooking

1 large green tomato, cut into four ½-inch (1.3-cm) slices

## FOR SANDWICHES

4 cups (120 g) packed baby spinach

4 English muffins, split and toasted

1 large ripe tomato, cut into four ½-inch (1.3-cm) slices

**TO MAKE THE DRESSING:** Combine the mayonnaise, bell pepper, garlic, horseradish, lemon juice, nutritional yeast, Worcestershire, sriracha, mustard, salt, and pepper in a blender. Blend until smooth. Stir in the scallion. Refrigerate in an airtight container until ready to use.

**TO MAKE THE FRIED GREEN TOMATOES:** Combine the milk, vinegar, horseradish, salt, and black pepper in a pie plate. Whisk to combine. In a second pie plate, combine the panko, cornmeal, and onion powder. Add salt and a generous pinch of pepper. Stir to combine. Place a paper towel on a plate for draining the tomatoes.

Heat ½ inch (1.3 cm) of oil in a large skillet over medium-high heat. Coat the tomato slices with the milk mixture, then dredge in the crumbs, patting the crumbs to adhere. Fry for 4 minutes, or until golden. Turn and cook the other side for 3 minutes. Drain on paper towels.

**TO ASSEMBLE THE SANDWICHES:** In a medium-size bowl, combine the spinach with ½ cup (106 g) of the dressing. Stir to coat. Spread the remaining dressing on the tops and bottoms of the English muffins. On the bottom, place the ripe tomato slice, the spinach, and the green tomato. Put the tops on and serve.

# PEPPERY TEMPEH SANDWICHES

Packed with spicy peppers and encompassed by a crusty roll, this sandwich delivers on depth of flavor. If you're a beer drinker, grab a cold one.

**YIELD**
4 SANDWICHES

### FOR MARINATED TEMPEH

2½ cups (590 ml) vegetable broth

¾ cup (180 ml) vegan beer

1 dried guajillo pepper

1 dried ancho pepper

1 dried chipotle pepper

1 lime, sliced

4 cloves garlic, sliced

3 tablespoons (45 ml) tamari

2 tablespoons (30 g) mustard

2 teaspoons pure maple syrup

2 teaspoons cumin seeds

2 teaspoons dried oregano

2 packages (8 ounces, or 227 g each) tempeh, cut lengthwise, then widthwise to get 4 patties out of each

### FOR SPREAD AND SANDWICHES

½ cup (112 g) vegan mayonnaise

2 tablespoons (30 ml) fresh lime juice

2 tablespoons (2 g) minced fresh cilantro

2 cloves garlic, minced

Salt and pepper, to taste

2 tablespoons plus 1 teaspoon (35 ml) canola oil, divided

3 cups (480 g) thinly sliced onion

Pinch of black pepper

2 tablespoons (18 g) minced jalapeño pepper

2 teaspoons balsamic vinegar

4 crusty rolls, cut in half and toasted

1 red bell pepper, cored and cut into strips

½ cucumber, sliced into thin rounds

**TO MAKE THE MARINATED TEMPEH:** Combine the broth, beer, peppers, lime, garlic, tamari, mustard, maple syrup, cumin, and oregano in a medium-size saucepan and bring to a boil over high heat. Reduce the heat and simmer for 30 minutes. Strain the marinade into a 9 x 13-inch (23 x 33-cm) baking dish. While the marinade is still hot, add the tempeh patties, turning to coat. Marinate in the refrigerator for 1 hour or longer.

**TO MAKE THE SPREAD:** Combine all the ingredients in a small bowl and mix well. Refrigerate in an airtight container until ready to use.

**TO ASSEMBLE THE SANDWICHES:** Preheat the oven to 300°F (150°C, or gas mark 2). In a large skillet, heat 1 teaspoon (5 ml) of the oil over medium-low heat. Add the onion and black pepper. Cook and stir for 15 minutes, until the onion has softened. Add the jalapeño and vinegar. Cook for 2 minutes longer, then keep warm.

Heat 1 tablespoon (15 ml) of the oil in another large skillet over medium heat. Cook 4 tempeh patties at a time for 4 minutes on one side, or until browned. Turn and cook the other side for 3 minutes. Pour half the marinade into the skillet. Cook for 8 minutes, or until the marinade has been absorbed. Keep cooked patties warm in the oven while cooking the second batch. Wipe the skillet clean and add the remaining 1 tablespoon (15 ml) oil, if needed. Cook the remaining 4 patties as before.

Smear the spread on both sides of each roll. Place 2 tempeh patties on each bottom half and layer with the bell pepper strips, cucumber, and sautéed onions. Put the tops on and serve.

# CARNITAS SANDWICHES

Jackfruit is a wonderful substitute for shredded meat because it has the perfect texture and absorbs the flavors of whatever sauce you marinate it in.

**YIELD**
4 SANDWICHES
1 SCANT CUP (215 G) CHILI CRÈME

### FOR CARNITAS

2 cans (20 ounces, or 565 g each) jackfruit in brine or water (not syrup)

½ cup (120 ml) fresh orange juice

2 tablespoons (14 g) onion powder

6 cloves garlic, minced, divided

3 tablespoons (45 ml) fresh lime juice, divided

¼ cup plus 2 tablespoons (90 ml) tamari, divided

1 tablespoon (15 ml) hot sauce

1 tablespoon (2 g) dried cilantro

1 teaspoon ground cumin

1 tablespoon (22 g) brown rice syrup

2 tablespoons (30 ml) olive oil

¼ cup (40 g) minced shallot

### FOR CHILI CRÈME

6 ounces (170 g) drained firm silken tofu

2 tablespoons (30 ml) olive oil

1 tablespoon (15 ml) fresh lime juice

½ teaspoon fine sea salt, to taste

1 teaspoon chili powder, to taste

½ teaspoon onion powder

1 tablespoon (1 g) chopped fresh cilantro

### FOR SANDWICHES

¾ cup (192 g) guacamole

4 sub sandwich rolls, 6 inches (15 cm) long, lightly toasted, or 4 individual baguettes, some of the inside removed, if needed

**TO MAKE THE CARNITAS:** Rinse, drain, and roughly shred the jackfruit.

Combine the jackfruit, orange juice, onion powder, 4 cloves of the garlic, 1 tablespoon (15 ml) of the lime juice, ¼ cup (60 ml) of the tamari, hot sauce, cilantro, cumin, and syrup in a large pot. Add enough water to reach about ¾ inch (2 cm) above the jackfruit. Cover and bring to a boil over high heat. Lower the heat and simmer for 1 hour, stirring occasionally. The jackfruit should still be fully immersed in liquid after the hour; stop simmering sooner if the liquid evaporates before. Do not drain. Let cool, cover, and chill the jackfruit in the liquid overnight, up to 24 hours.

When ready to cook, drain the jackfruit. Heat the oil in a large skillet over medium-high heat. Add the jackfruit, the remaining 2 cloves garlic, and the shallot. Cook for 10 minutes, or until the jackfruit starts to brown. Stir occasionally. Add the remaining 2 tablespoons (30 ml) lime juice and remaining 2 tablespoons (30 ml) tamari, and cook for 5 minutes longer. Set aside.

**TO MAKE THE CRÈME:** Combine all the ingredients in a food processor and process until smooth, scraping the sides with a rubber spatula as needed. Store in an airtight container in the fridge for up to 1 week.

**TO ASSEMBLE THE SANDWICHES:** Spread 3 tablespoons (48 g) guacamole on one half of each roll. Spread 2 generous tablespoons (36 g) chili crème on the other side of each roll. Pile ½ cup (100 g) packed, warm jackfruit on top, or enough to fit the size of the roll without spilling over. Cut in half, for less mess, and serve immediately.

# ASIAN EGGPLANT SANDWICHES

Crunchy slaw is the perfect topper to the sweet and spicy glazed eggplant. This one can be on the table in minutes and is sure to beat take-out. If sambal oelek is unavailable, sriracha is a great substitute.

**YIELD**
4 SANDWICHES

### FOR SALAD

2 cups (140 g) shredded napa cabbage

¼ cup (40 g) sliced red onion

2 tablespoons (14 g) grated carrot

1½ teaspoons seasoned rice vinegar

Pinch of black pepper

### FOR SAUCE

¼ cup (60 g) ketchup

2 tablespoons (30 ml) tamari

2 tablespoons (30 ml) seasoned rice vinegar

1 tablespoon plus 1 teaspoon (20 g) sambal oelek, to taste

2 teaspoons smooth peanut butter

### FOR EGGPLANT

2 teaspoons toasted sesame oil

1 large eggplant, cut into ½-inch (1.3-cm) rounds, then quartered

2 cloves garlic, minced

1 teaspoon grated fresh ginger

1½ teaspoons toasted sesame seeds

Salt and pepper, to taste

### FOR SANDWICHES

¼ cup (56 g) vegan mayonnaise

1 baguette, 20 inches (51 cm) long, cut in half lengthwise, some of the inside removed, and toasted

**TO MAKE THE SALAD:** Combine all the ingredients in a medium-size bowl.

**TO MAKE THE SAUCE:** Whisk together all the ingredients in a small bowl.

**TO MAKE THE EGGPLANT:** Heat the sesame oil in a large skillet over medium heat. Add the eggplant. Cook, stirring, for 6 minutes, or until it begins to soften. Add the garlic and ginger and cook for 2 minutes, stirring. Stir in the sauce and the sesame seeds. Taste and adjust the seasoning with salt and pepper. Cook for 2 minutes longer, or until heated through.

**TO ASSEMBLE THE SANDWICHES:** Spread the mayonnaise on the bottom of the baguette and layer on the eggplant and salad. Replace the top and cut into 4 equal pieces.

### SERVING SUGGESTIONS AND VARIATIONS

Six large portobello mushrooms, stemmed, gilled, and cut into ½-inch (1.3-cm) slices may be substituted for the eggplant. The rest of the recipe remains the same.

# CHICKPEA SHAWARMA

There's nothing chickpeas can't do! We won't go into details about what type of meats are typically used in this Middle Eastern kind of taco; suffice it to say that this version is a healthy meal that won't leave you feeling as though you're depriving yourself. That's what it's all about.

**YIELD**
4 SANDWICHES
1 ⅓ CUPS (315 ML) DRESSING

## FOR CHICKPEAS

1 tablespoon (15 ml) apple cider vinegar

1 tablespoon (15 ml) fresh lemon juice

2 tablespoons (30 g) unsweetened plain nondairy yogurt

1 tablespoon (15 ml) olive oil

Salt and pepper, to taste

2 cloves garlic, pressed

1 teaspoon onion powder

1 teaspoon mild to medium curry powder

1 can (15 ounces, or 425 g) chickpeas, drained and rinsed

## FOR TAHINI DRESSING

½ cup (128 g) tahini

¼ cup (60 g) unsweetened plain nondairy yogurt

¼ cup (60 ml) water

¼ cup (60 ml) fresh lemon juice

2 tablespoons (30 ml) olive oil

1 or 2 cloves garlic, pressed, to taste

Salt and pepper, to taste

3 tablespoons (30 g) chopped red onion

## FOR SANDWICHES

2 cups (144 g) shredded lettuce

Four 8-inch (20 cm) pita breads, lightly toasted

4 small tomatoes, chopped

¼ cup (15 g) chopped fresh parsley

Lemon wedges, for serving

**TO MAKE THE CHICKPEAS:** Preheat the oven to 350°F (180°C, or gas mark 4). Combine the vinegar, lemon juice, yogurt, oil, salt, pepper, garlic, onion powder, and curry powder in a 9-inch (23-cm) baking dish. Add the chickpeas, stir to coat well, and bake for 20 minutes, until the liquid has been mostly absorbed. Set aside.

**TO MAKE THE TAHINI DRESSING:** Combine the tahini, yogurt, water, lemon juice, oil, garlic, salt, and pepper in a blender. Blend until smooth. Stir in the onion. Store in an airtight container in the fridge for up to 1 week. If it thickens after refrigeration, add as much water, lemon juice, and salt as needed to thin it out and to keep the flavor profile bright. You will have some dressing left over; save it for another use.

**TO ASSEMBLE THE SANDWICHES:** Place ½ cup (36 g) lettuce on each pita bread. On top of each, add 1 small chopped tomato and a generous ⅓ cup (85 g) chickpeas. Drizzle with as much dressing as desired. Sprinkle each pita with 1 table-spoon (4 g) chopped parsley. Fold your pita as best you can, taco style. Serve with the lemon wedges.

### SERVING SUGGESTIONS AND VARIATIONS

If you prefer, stuff the breads with just the filling instead, for less messy results, or use flour tortillas and make these as wraps.

# OUT OF TUNA SANDWICHES

This is a take on salad niçoise, which is named for the city of Nice in France. We made it in sandwich-form, which is even *nicer* because it says no to tuna and anchovies.

**YIELD**
3 SANDWICHES

## FOR CHICKPEA TUNA

1 can (15 ounces, or 425 g) chickpeas, drained and rinsed

½ cup (120 g) miso dressing (page 107)

2 teaspoons fresh lemon juice

½ teaspoon minced capers

1 teaspoon Dijon mustard

1 teaspoon minced shallot

½ teaspoon kelp powder

⅛ teaspoon dried dillweed

Salt and pepper, to taste

## FOR DRESSING

Salt and pepper, to taste

1 small clove garlic, pressed

2 teaspoons fresh lemon juice

2 teaspoons white balsamic vinegar

½ teaspoon Dijon mustard

2 tablespoons (30 ml) extra-virgin olive oil

2 teaspoons minced shallot

1 teaspoon capers, drained and chopped

½ teaspoon vegan Worcestershire sauce

## FOR SANDWICHES

3 soft bread rolls, cut in half, or 6 slices sandwich bread, lightly toasted

18 small yellow leaves from heart of romaine

6 thin slices tomato

6 ounces (170 g) green beans, cooked until crisp-tender

12 olives of choice, for serving

**TO MAKE THE CHICKPEA TUNA:** Pulse the chickpeas in a food processor a few times, not to purée, but just not to have all the beans left whole. Transfer to a large bowl and add the remaining ingredients. Stir to combine. Cover with plastic wrap and refrigerate for about 2 hours.

**TO MAKE THE DRESSING:** Combine all the ingredients in a small bowl and whisk thoroughly. Whisk again just before using.

**TO ASSEMBLE THE SANDWICHES:** Place ½ cup (120 g) chickpea tuna on the bottom of each roll. Top with 6 lettuce leaves and 2 tomato slices. Combine the green beans with the (freshly whisked) dressing. Place 2 ounces (a little under ½ cup, or 57 g) of beans on top of the tomato slices. Replace the top of the roll and serve immediately alongside 4 olives (or more, if desired) per serving.

# PAN BAGNAT

This may be the ultimate picnic sandwich. Best made ahead, it transports easily and is made even better when matched with a bottle of white wine. Prepare the dressing first to give the flavors time to meld. French in origin, the name means "bathed bread" in Provençal dialect.

| | YIELD |
|---|---|
| | 4 SANVDWICHES |

**FOR DRESSING**

Generous pinch of dried basil

Generous pinch of dried parsley

Generous pinch of black pepper

Pinch of red pepper flakes

¼ teaspoon fine sea salt

1 clove garlic, minced

1½ tablespoons (25 ml) red wine vinegar

1 teaspoon Dijon mustard

½ teaspoon agave nectar

4½ tablespoons (68 ml) olive oil

**FOR SANDWICHES**

3 artichoke hearts (packed in water), drained, patted dry, and minced

⅓ cup (34 g) chopped niçoise olives

½ teaspoon olive oil

2 large portobello caps, stemmed, gilled, and cut into ½-inch (1.3-cm) slices

½ teaspoon fresh lemon juice

Salt and pepper, to taste

1 baguette, 16 inches (40 cm) long, cut in half lengthwise and some of the inside removed

Lettuce leaves

Handful fresh basil leaves

1 tomato, thinly sliced

6 spears asparagus, steamed until tender

1 thin slice red onion, cut into half-moons

2 radishes, thinly sliced

**TO MAKE THE DRESSING:** Whisk together the basil, parsley, black pepper, red pepper flakes, salt, garlic, and vinegar in a small bowl until the salt dissolves. Add the mustard, agave, and oil and whisk until thickened. Refrigerate in an airtight container until ready to use.

**TO MAKE THE SANDWICHES:** Stir the artichokes and olives together in a small bowl to make tapenade.

Heat the oil in a large skillet over medium heat. Add the mushrooms and cook, stirring, until they begin to release their juices, about 5 minutes. Remove from the heat, add the lemon juice and season with salt and pepper.

Pour a generous tablespoon (20 ml) of dressing on the bottom of the baguette. Layer with the lettuce, basil, tomato, and mushrooms. Top with the asparagus, red onion, and radishes. Layer the tapenade evenly on top. Drizzle the remaining dressing on the inside of the top and place on the sandwich. Press the sandwich closed. Wrap tightly in foil. To serve soon, press the wrapped sandwich under a cutting board topped with a cast-iron skillet for 10 minutes. While still wrapped, cut the sandwich into 4 pieces. To serve later, refrigerate until serving without pressing.

**SERVING SUGGESTIONS AND VARIATIONS**

Instead of a baguette, make this one on ciabatta rolls for easy packing and serving.

# CURRIED CHICKPEA & CHUTNEY PITA PARTY

Sweet and savory foods make the world go 'round, and if you're anything like us, you might find yourself piling a whole jar of the chutney on top of the curried chickpea filling. Oops. It's that good.

| YIELD |
|:---:|
| 6 SANDWICHES, |
| 3 CUPS (700 G) CHUTNEY |

### FOR CHUTNEY

5 cups (770 g) halved, pitted, and diced peaches or nectarines

1 tablespoon (5 g) ground ginger

½ teaspoon fine sea salt

¼ teaspoon red pepper flakes

1 teaspoon garam masala

½ cup (100 g) loosely packed brown sugar

½ cup (100 g) granulated sugar

1 cup (235 ml) apple cider vinegar

½ cup (120 ml) water

### FOR CURRIED CHICKPEAS

1 cup (240 g) unsweetened plain nondairy yogurt

2 tablespoons (30 ml) fresh lemon juice

2 cloves garlic, grated

2 tablespoons (20 g) chopped scallion or red onion

2 teaspoons mild to medium curry powder

½ teaspoon fine sea salt, to taste

⅓ cup (45 g) dry-roasted cashews, chopped

½ cup (80 g) petite green peas, cooked

2 cups (480 g) cooked chickpeas

### FOR SANDWICHES

1½ cups (30 g) baby arugula or baby spinach

Six 8-inch (20 cm) pita breads, split open

**TO MAKE THE CHUTNEY:** Place all the ingredients in a large pot. Bring to a boil, uncovered, and simmer for 60 to 90 minutes over medium heat, stirring occasionally, until thickened. Store in an airtight container in the fridge and enjoy within a month.

**TO MAKE THE CURRIED CHICKPEAS:** Combine the yogurt, lemon juice, garlic, scallion, curry powder, and salt in a medium-size bowl and stir well. Add the cashews, peas, and chickpeas, stirring to combine. Refrigerate for at least 1 hour to let the flavors develop.

**TO ASSEMBLE THE SANDWICHES:** Place ¼ cup (5 g) arugula in an opened pita pocket, top with ½ cup (123 g) chickpeas and add 2 tablespoons (30 g) or more chutney on top. Serve.

# PAV BHAJI

Pav bhaji is a popular street food dish in India, consisting of a thick potato-based curry (bhaji) and soft rolls (pav)—sort of like sloppy joes, only way kinder and way spicier.

If you have a hard time finding pav bhaji masala even at an international market, make this with garam masala instead. It won't be authentic, but we've made it both ways and loved them equally.

**POTENTIALLY**

| YIELD |
| --- |
| 8 SANDWICHES |

1 large white potato (10 ounces, or 280 g), diced

2 heaping cups (290 g) frozen cauliflower florets

2 tablespoons (30 ml) olive oil

⅓ cup (50 g) chopped red onion

1 small hot green pepper, seeded and minced

1 red bell pepper, cored and diced

2 cloves garlic, pressed

1 to 1½ teaspoons grated fresh ginger, to taste

¼ teaspoon turmeric

1 tablespoon (5 g) pav bhaji masala

1 cup (260 g) crushed tomatoes

½ cup (80 g) cooked petite green peas

Salt, to taste

Nondairy butter, for rolls

8 large soft rolls, cut in half and lightly toasted

½ cup (8 g) chopped fresh cilantro

Place the potato and cauliflower florets in a large pot and cover with water. Bring to a boil over high heat and cook until tender, 10 to 15 minutes, then drain. Mash and set aside.

Heat the oil in a large skillet over medium-high heat, add the onion, green pepper, and bell pepper and cook until tender, about 5 minutes. Add the garlic, ginger, turmeric, and masala and cook for 1 minute longer. Add the tomatoes, peas, and salt to taste. Add the mashed potato and florets, stir well, cover with a lid, and simmer on low heat for 15 minutes, stirring occasionally. The mixture should be very thick but not dry, so if it gets dry before the cooking is done, add a little water or vegetable broth to moisten it just a bit.

To assemble the sandwiches, lightly butter both halves of the rolls. Scoop ½ cup (120 g) pav bhaji on the bottom half. Sprinkle with 1 tablespoon (1 g) chopped cilantro. Replace the top, or leave open-faced, and serve immediately.

**SERVING SUGGESTIONS AND VARIATIONS**

• We also like to serve this on a bun covered with a thin layer of simply dressed, mayo-free coleslaw for a bit of extra vegetable goodness and crunch.

• This is a recipe that's rather messy, so have napkins handy! Or eat it open-faced with a fork and knife, if you really must.

# KATI ROLLS

These spicy Indian wraps are easy to make, but if you're pressed for time (or just plain lazy) and don't feel like making the chapatis from scratch, you can find ready-made vegan paratha, chapati, or roti at most international markets. Just remember to check the ingredients!

**YIELD**
16 ROLLS

### FOR CHAPATIS

2 cups (240 g) whole wheat flour

2 cups (250 g) all-purpose flour

2 teaspoons sugar

1½ teaspoons fine sea salt, to taste

Pepper, to taste

¼ cup (60 ml) olive oil

2 cups (470 ml) unsweetened plain nondairy milk, warmed, as needed

Nonstick cooking spray

### FOR FILLING

2 tablespoons (30 ml) peanut oil

2 small potatoes, cut into small dice

½ cup (80 g) chopped scallion

3 medium-size tomatoes, diced

1 cup (149 g) cored, seeded, and diced red, yellow, or orange bell pepper

2 cloves garlic, pressed

1 to 2 teaspoons grated fresh ginger

1 teaspoon garam masala

½ teaspoon ground coriander

½ teaspoon ground cumin

¼ teaspoon turmeric

¼ to ½ teaspoon cayenne pepper, to taste (optional)

8 ounces (227 g) super-firm tofu, cut into ⅓-inch (8-mm) cubes

¼ cup (60 ml) water

Salt and pepper, to taste

Chutney, for serving (optional)

**TO MAKE THE CHAPATIS:** Combine the flours, sugar, salt, and pepper in a large bowl. Add the oil and the milk, a little at a time for the latter, as needed. Knead until the dough is soft and smooth. Let rest for 15 minutes.

Divide the dough into 16 portions, and roll them out thinly (like tortillas) on a lightly floured surface.

Lightly coat a griddle with cooking spray, preheat to medium-high, and cook each chapati until brown spots form, about 1 to 2 minutes per side. Place each chapati on a plate, on top of each other, while cooking the rest. Set aside while preparing the filling.

**TO MAKE THE FILLING:** Heat the oil in a large skillet over medium heat. Add the diced potatoes and cook until barely tender, about 8 minutes. Add the scallion, tomatoes, and bell pepper, and cook until just tender, about 4 minutes. Add the garlic, ginger, and all the spices and cook for 1 minute longer. Add the tofu cubes and let brown for about 6 minutes. Add the water, salt, and pepper and cook for about 4 minutes, or until the water has been absorbed.

**TO ASSEMBLE THE KATI ROLLS:** Place one chapati on a plate, spread ¼ cup (48 g) filling in a line down the center, and fold the chapati over the filling. Wrap the ends in foil for a less messy eating experience. Serve with the chutney.

# BÁNH MÌ

Originating during the French colonization of Vietnam, this sandwich has many variations. We chose spiced seitan, which contrasts beautifully with the crisp, Asian-seasoned vegetables.

**YIELD**
4 SANDWICHES

### FOR PICKLED VEGETABLES

3 tablespoons (45 ml) water

3 tablespoons (45 ml) white vinegar

2 tablespoons (25 g) sugar

½ cup (85 g) julienned carrot

½ cup (85 g) julienned daikon radish

¼ cup (113 g) julienned baby bok choy (white part only)

3 tablespoons (18 g) minced scallion

1 teaspoon fresh lime juice

Salt, to taste

### FOR SEITAN AND SANDWICHES

Nonstick cooking spray

12 ounces (340 g) Moo-Free Seitan, cut into ¼-inch (6-mm) slices (page 180)

3 tablespoons (45 ml) vegetable broth

1 teaspoon tamari

1 teaspoon seasoned rice vinegar

½ to 1 teaspoon sambal oelek or sriracha, to taste

½ teaspoon toasted sesame oil

1 tablespoon (10 g) minced shallot

1 clove garlic, minced

½ teaspoon five-spice powder

Salt and pepper, to taste

¼ cup (56 g) vegan mayonnaise

1 baguette, 24 inches (60 cm) long, cut lengthwise, some of the inside removed to hold the filling, and toasted

½ English cucumber, thinly sliced

½ jalapeño pepper, thinly sliced

Handful cilantro leaves

**TO MAKE THE PICKLED VEGETABLES:** Bring the water, vinegar, and sugar to a boil in a small saucepan. Remove from the heat. Combine the vegetables and liquid in a medium-size bowl. Stir. Add the lime juice and salt to taste. Refrigerate in an airtight container for 1 hour or longer.

**TO MAKE THE FILLING:** Heat a grill pan over medium-high heat. Spray with nonstick spray. Grill the seitan slices for 4 minutes per side, or until marked. Combine the broth, tamari, vinegar, and sambal oelek in a small bowl. Place the seitan on a cutting board and cut into ½-inch (1.3-cm) strips. Heat the oil in a large skillet over medium heat. Add the shallot, garlic, and five-spice powder. Cook, stirring, for 2 to 3 minutes, or until fragrant. Add the seitan strips and broth mixture. Cook, stirring, for 4 minutes, or until the liquid has been absorbed. Season to taste with salt and pepper.

**TO ASSEMBLE THE SANDWICHES:** Spread 2 tablespoons (28 g) of the mayonnaise on each side of the baguette. Layer with the seitan, cucumbers, jalapeños, and cilantro. With a slotted spoon, scoop the vegetables from the dressing and spread evenly on top. Replace the top of the baguette and cut into 4 pieces.

### SERVING SUGGESTIONS AND VARIATIONS

With the parts packed separately, this one is ideal to assemble when you get to your destination. Just be sure to keep the mayo cool.

# TORTA DE TOFU

Spicy, savory tofu is stacked on a baguette with vegetables and seasoned mayonnaise and accented with avocado slices. Increase the chipotle in the marinade for even more South of the Border heat *(pictured on page 2)*.

| | YIELD |
|---|---|
| | 4 SANDWICHES |

**FOR SAUCE**

½ cup (112 g) vegan mayonnaise

2 tablespoons (30 g) mustard

1 tablespoon (8 g) nutritional yeast

**FOR MARINATED TOFU**

1 chipotle pepper in adobo sauce, minced

2 cloves garlic, minced

1 tablespoon (10 g) minced shallot

3 tablespoons (45 ml) dry red wine

¾ cup (180 ml) vegetable broth

1 tablespoon (15 ml) tamari

1 teaspoon blackstrap molasses

½ teaspoon ground cumin

½ teaspoon dried oregano

Generous pinch of fine sea salt

Generous pinch of black pepper

1 pound (454 g) extra-firm tofu, drained, pressed, and cut into 8 pieces

2 teaspoons olive oil

**FOR SANDWICHES**

1 baguette, 18 inches (46 cm) long, sliced in half lengthwise, some of the inside removed, and toasted

¼ cup (36 g) pickled jalapeño slices

4 thin slices red onion, cut into half-moons

1 green bell pepper, cored and cut into strips

1 avocado, pitted, peeled, and sliced

**TO MAKE THE SAUCE:** Combine all the ingredients in a blender. Blend until smooth. Refrigerate in an airtight container until ready to use.

**TO MAKE THE MARINATED TOFU:** Combine the chipotle, garlic, shallot, wine, broth, tamari, molasses, cumin, oregano, salt, and pepper in a 9 x 13-inch (23 x 33-cm) pan. Place the tofu in the marinade and turn to coat. Cover and refrigerate, turning occasionally, for at least 1 hour.

Preheat the oven to 425°F (220°C, or gas mark 7). Bake the tofu in the pan for 15 minutes. Turn the tofu over and bake for 10 minutes longer, or until all the marinade has been absorbed.

Turn the oven to broil. Brush the tops of the tofu with the olive oil and broil for 2 to 3 minutes, or until crisp.

**TO ASSEMBLE THE SANDWICHES:** Spread the sauce evenly on the cut sides of the baguette. Place the tofu on the bread. Top evenly with the jalapeños, red onion, bell pepper, and avocado. Put the top on the baguette. Cut into 4 pieces and serve.

**SERVING SUGGESTIONS AND VARIATIONS**

• For a side dish, add some sweet potato fries.

• Make extra sauce to keep on hand. Slather it on burgers for some tangy goodness

# JIMWICH

Jim, Tami's husband, is a sandwich lover and when he was given a chance to imagine his signature sandwich, this was it. Jim thinks outside the box, and we dare you to try to box this one. With fried pickles on a sandwich, how wrong can it be? Some of the best sandwiches are a little messy, so be prepared.

**YIELD**
4 SANDWICHES

## FOR SEITAN

1 pound (454 g) Moo-Free Seitan (page 180), thinly sliced

½ cup (120 ml) dry red wine

½ teaspoon black pepper

½ teaspoon smoked salt

## FOR BARBECUED ONIONS AND DRESSING

1 teaspoon olive oil

1¼ cups (200 g) thinly sliced onion

3 tablespoons (48 g) barbecue sauce, homemade (page 123) or store-bought

⅓ cup (75 g) vegan mayonnaise

1 tablespoon (15 g) mustard

2 teaspoons hot sauce

2 teaspoons white wine vinegar

## FOR FRIED PICKLES

1¼ cups (194 g) dill pickles cut into ½-inch (1.3-cm) rounds and patted dry

6 tablespoons (48 g) all-purpose flour, divided

Canola oil, for cooking

½ cup (120 ml) nondairy milk

½ teaspoon baking powder

¼ teaspoon smoked paprika

## FOR SEITAN AND SANDWICHES

1 baguette, 20 inches (50 cm) long, halved lengthwise and some of the inside removed

2 cups (140 g) shredded lettuce

1 large tomato, sliced

**TO MAKE THE SEITAN:** Preheat the oven to 400°F (200°C, or gas mark 6). Combine the seitan, wine, pepper, and salt in a 9 x 13-inch (23 x 33-cm) pan. Bake for 10 minutes, or until the liquid has evaporated.

**TO MAKE THE ONIONS:** Heat the oil in a large skillet over medium heat. Add the onion and cook, stirring, for 10 minutes, or until softened. Stir in the sauce. Cook for 2 minutes longer. Set aside and keep warm.

**TO MAKE THE DRESSING:** Mix all the ingredients together in a small bowl until smooth.

**TO MAKE THE PICKLES:** Line a plate with paper towels. In a medium-size bowl, toss the pickles with 1 tablespoon (8 g) of the flour. Pour ¼ inch (6 mm) oil into a large skillet and heat over medium-high heat. In a pie plate, stir together the milk, remaining 5 tablespoons (40 g) flour, baking powder, and paprika. Working in batches, dip the floured pickles into the batter, then place in the skillet. Cook for 3 minutes, or until golden. Turn and cook the other side for 2 minutes. Transfer to the plate to drain.

**TO ASSEMBLE THE SANDWICHES:** Spread the dressing evenly on both sides of the bread. Layer with the seitan, onions, pickles, lettuce, and tomato; replace the top of the bread. Cut into 4 pieces and serve.

# MARINATED EGGPLANT SANDWICHES

Chewy, baked tofu slices paired with insanely addictive and spicy (but not in a "Call the fire brigade, my tongue is burning!" kind of way) eggplant? You've got yourself a deal. And a meal.

**YIELD**
4 SANDWICHES
ABOUT 40 SLICES EGGPLANT

### FOR MARINATED EGGPLANT

1 small (14 ounces, or 400 g) eggplant, cut in half widthwise, then cut lengthwise into ¼-inch (6-mm)-thick slices

¼ cup (60 ml) olive oil, divided

2 tablespoons (30 ml) apple cider vinegar

2 teaspoons Cajun spice mix

2 teaspoons vegan Worcestershire sauce

½ teaspoon liquid smoke

### FOR TOFU

¼ cup (60 ml) white balsamic vinegar

2 tablespoons (30 ml) olive oil

2 tablespoons (15 g) nutritional yeast

1 teaspoon onion powder

2 cloves garlic, pressed

Salt and pepper, to taste

1 pound (454 g) super-firm or extra-firm tofu, drained, pressed, and cut lengthwise into four ¼-inch (6-mm) steaks

### FOR SANDWICHES

½ cup (112 g) vegan mayonnaise

4 sub sandwich rolls or mini baguettes, 6 inches (15 cm) long, cut in half and lightly toasted

1⅓ cups (96 g) shredded lettuce

**TO MAKE THE MARINATED EGGPLANT:** Preheat the broiler to 450°F (230°C, or gas mark 8). Place the eggplant on one or two large baking sheets. In a small bowl, combine 2 tablespoons (30 ml) of the olive oil with the vinegar and Cajun spice mix. Lightly brush this mixture on both sides of the eggplant slices. Broil for 4 minutes on each side, or until dark brown. In the meantime, in another small bowl, combine the remaining 2 tablespoons (30 ml) olive oil with the Worcestershire sauce and liquid smoke.

Carefully remove the baking sheet from the oven. Brush both sides of the eggplant slices with the Worcestershire mixture and let them cool on a wire rack. Let stand for at least 30 minutes before serving, or even better, up to overnight. Store leftovers in an airtight container in the fridge for up to 4 days. To get the best out of the flavors, bring back to room temperature before serving.

**TO MAKE THE TOFU:** Combine the vinegar, oil, nutritional yeast, onion powder, garlic, salt, and pepper in a large rectangular shallow dish. Add the tofu and turn to coat thoroughly; let marinate for 30 minutes.

Decrease the oven temperature to 425°F (220°C, or gas mark 7). Bake the tofu for 30 minutes, flipping once halfway through. Note that the tofu will become chewier once cooled.

**TO ASSEMBLE THE SANDWICHES:** Spread 1 tablespoon (14 g) mayonnaise on each side of the roll. Place ⅓ cup (24 g) shredded lettuce on top. Place 1 tofu slice on each sandwich and place 4 to 6 slices marinated eggplant on top. Serve immediately.

# APRICOT FENNEL SANDWICHES

We think it's time to give fennel the appreciation it deserves, and we believe this unusual (in a good way!) sandwich will be a great introduction to those who might be a little suspicious of the truly fantastic aromatic bulb.

**YIELD**
4 SANDWICHES
¾ CUP (225 G) SPREAD

**FOR SPREAD**

6 ounces (170 g) drained firm silken tofu

2 tablespoons (30 ml) capers with brine

3 tablespoons (45 ml) olive oil

½ teaspoon cayenne pepper, to taste

1 tablespoon (15 ml) fresh lemon juice

Zest of ½ lemon

2 cloves garlic, grated

Pinch of salt, to taste

**FOR FENNEL**

1 tablespoon (15 ml) olive oil

1 bulb (10 ounces, or 280 g) fennel, trimmed and thinly sliced lengthwise

2 cloves garlic, minced

1 tablespoon (10 g) minced shallot

1 tablespoon (21 g) agave nectar

¼ teaspoon fine sea salt, to taste

**FOR TEMPEH**

1 tablespoon (15 ml) tamari

2 tablespoons (40 g) all-fruit apricot jam

1 tablespoon (15 ml) fresh lemon juice

1 tablespoon (15 ml) olive oil

8 ounces (227 g) tempeh, cut into ⅓-inch (8-mm) cubes

4 apricots, halved, pitted, and chopped

**FOR SANDWICHES**

8 fresh basil leaves, minced

4 crusty rolls, cut in half

Salt and pepper, to taste

**TO MAKE THE SPREAD:** Combine all the ingredients in a food processor. Process until smooth. Transfer to an airtight container and chill in the fridge for 1 hour.

**TO MAKE THE FENNEL:** Heat the oil in a skillet over medium heat. Add the fennel and increase the heat to medium-high, then add the garlic, shallot, and agave and stir to combine. Cook for just about 5 minutes, stirring frequently. The fennel should remain crunchy and barely start to caramelize. Remove from the heat. Add the salt and stir to combine. Transfer to a bowl and use the same pan to prepare the tempeh.

**TO MAKE THE TEMPEH:** Whisk the tamari, jam, and lemon juice together in a small bowl. Set aside. Heat the oil in the skillet over medium-high heat. Add the tempeh cubes and cook, stirring often, until golden brown, about 4 minutes. Add the chopped apricots and reserved sauce and cook until the glaze coats the tempeh and the liquid has been absorbed, about 2 minutes.

**TO ASSEMBLE THE SANDWICHES:** Stir the basil into the spread. Smear a generous 1½ tablespoons (28 g) spread on each half of the rolls. Top with ⅓ cup (50 g) packed fennel and a heaping ⅓ cup (80 g) tempeh. Sprinkle with extra salt and pepper, if desired. Replace the top half of the rolls and serve.

# CHOW MEIN SANDWICHES

We put our own spin on a crazy sandwich that usually involves a different type of sauce made with molasses. We occasionally like to serve this one with a couple of baked (or grilled) tofu slices, for added protein on top of those carbs.

**FOR PASTA**

2 packages (4.4 ounces, or 125 g) vegan chow mein noodles

1 tablespoon (15 ml) peanut oil

**FOR VEGETABLES**

1 tablespoon (15 ml) sesame or peanut oil

4 stalks center yellow part of celery heart, thinly sliced

1 green or red bell pepper, cored and cut into thin strips

½ cup (80 g) thinly sliced (into half-moons) red onion

4 cloves garlic, minced

1 cup (104 g) mung bean sprouts

**FOR SAUCE**

¾ cup (180 ml) pineapple juice

¼ cup (60 ml) tamari

2 tablespoons (30 ml) apple cider vinegar

¼ cup (60 ml) vegetable broth

1 to 2 teaspoons sriracha, to taste

2 tablespoons (16 g) cornstarch

Salt, to taste

**FOR SANDWICHES**

4 burger buns, cut in half and lightly toasted

**TO MAKE THE PASTA:** Bring 8 cups (1.9L) water to a boil in a large pot, add the nests of pasta, and cook, following the package instructions, until just tender, usually about 4 minutes. Drain well and let cool completely before using. Reserve the pan for making the sauce.

Once the pasta is completely cooled, heat the oil in a large skillet over medium heat and divide the cold pasta into 4 individual nests: they will be stiff and uncooperative. Fry the nests as single units until golden brown and crispy, about 10 minutes, flipping once halfway through and watching the heat so the pasta doesn't burn. Transfer to a wire rack.

**TO MAKE THE VEGETABLES:** Return the skillet to the stove, add the oil and heat over medium-high heat. Add the celery, bell pepper, onion, and garlic. Cook for 2 to 3 minutes, until the vegetables are crisp-tender. Stir in the mung bean sprouts and cook for 1 minute longer. Set aside.

**TO MAKE THE SAUCE:** Return the medium-size saucepan to the stove and add the pineapple juice, tamari, vinegar, broth, and sriracha. In a separate small bowl, combine 1/4 cup (60 ml) of this mixture with the cornstarch, stirring to dissolve. Set aside. Bring the pineapple juice mixture to a boil, lower the heat to medium-high, and cook for 2 minutes to meld the flavors. Add the cornstarch slurry to thicken the sauce, stirring constantly, and remove from the heat when the sauce is thick, 1 to 2 minutes. Pour the sauce over the vegetables and stir to combine. Season with salt, if needed.

**TO ASSEMBLE THE SANDWICHES:** Place each pasta nest on the bottom half of each burger bun. Top with a generous amount of the vegetables and sauce. Top with the other half of the bun.

# JAMAICAN DIP

The flavors of the island captured on a bun! With both a marinade and a rub, the two-step seasoning infuses these cutlets with flavor. Serve with a side of reggae.

### FOR MARINATED CUTLETS

2¼ cups (530 ml) vegetable broth

2 dried habanero peppers

1 large jalapeño pepper, stemmed and seeded

¾ cup (75 g) 1-inch (2.5-cm) pieces scallion

3-inch (7.5-cm) cinnamon stick

1½ teaspoons dried thyme

¼ cup (60 ml) fresh lemon juice

3 tablespoons (45 ml) fresh lime juice

3 tablespoons (45 ml) tamari

4 cloves garlic, sliced

1 bay leaf

¾-inch (1-cm) piece ginger, sliced

1½ tablespoons (23 g) packed light brown sugar

1 teaspoon blackstrap molasses

4 No Cluck Cutlets (page 181)

### FOR RUB AND SANDWICHES

1 teaspoon dried thyme

1 teaspoon dried sage

½ teaspoon ground allspice

½ teaspoon black pepper

¼ teaspoon cayenne pepper

⅛ teaspoon ground cinnamon

⅛ teaspoon fine sea salt

Pinch of ground nutmeg

Nonstick cooking spray

4 hoagie buns, cut in half and some of the inside removed

**TO MAKE THE MARINATED CUTLETS:** Combine the broth, peppers, scallion, cinnamon stick, thyme, lemon and lime juices, tamari, garlic, bay leaf, ginger, brown sugar, and molasses in a medium saucepan and bring to a boil over high heat. Decrease the heat to low and simmer for 20 minutes. Drain through a mesh strainer into a 9 x 13-inch (23 x 33-cm) pan. Add the cutlets, turning to coat. Marinate in the refrigerator for 1 hour or longer. Drain the cutlets, reserving the marinade.

**TO MAKE THE RUB:** Combine all the ingredients on a plate. Rub into both sides of the marinated cutlets.

**TO ASSEMBLE THE SANDWICHES:** Heat the reserved marinade in a small saucepan. Keep warm. Heat a grill pan over medium-high heat. Coat with nonstick spray. Grill the cutlets for 5 minutes, or until marked on one side. Turn and cook the other side for 4 minutes, or until marked. Transfer to a cutting board and cut into strips. Place the strips on the buns. Top each with ¼ cup (63 g) salsa. Remove the cinnamon stick, ginger, and bay leaf from the reserved marinade and serve on the side for dipping.

**TO MAKE SALSA:** (We like this with salsa.) In a small bowl, mix together ¼ cup (25 g) minced scallion, 1 kiwi, peeled and diced, ¼ cup (40 g) diced pineapple, 1 teaspoon minced fresh thyme, 1 teaspoon seasoned rice vinegar, pinch of black pepper, and ¼ cup (35 g) diced cucumber. Spoon on top of the seitan strips.

# SALVADORIAN SEITAN AND BEAN SANDWICHES

This easy-to-make sandwich packs a punch with its complex South American nuances. It's a little citrusy, a little spicy, and all wonderful.

**YIELD**
4 SANDWICHES

## FOR MARINATED SEITAN

3 tablespoons (45 ml) rum or vegetable broth

2 tablespoons (30 ml) fresh lime juice

2 tablespoons (30 ml) fresh orange juice

2 teaspoons tamari

1 tablespoon (15 g) ketchup

1 tablespoon (10 g) minced red onion

1 clove garlic, minced

2 teaspoons ground cumin

1 teaspoon ground coriander

½ teaspoon red pepper flakes

12 ounces (340 g) Moo-Free Seitan (page 180), cut into ¼-inch (6-mm) slices

Nonstick cooking spray

## FOR SANDWICHES

2 teaspoons olive oil

¼ cup (40 g) minced red onion

1 teaspoon ground cumin

2 cloves garlic, minced

1 can (15 ounces, or 425 g) black beans, drained and rinsed

3 tablespoons (45 ml) reserved marinade

Salt and pepper, to taste

4 kaiser or other rolls, cut in half and toasted

¼ cup (56 g) vegan mayonnaise

**TO MAKE THE MARINATED SEITAN:** Blend the rum, lime and orange juices, tamari, ketchup, onion, garlic, cumin, coriander, and red pepper flakes in a blender until smooth. Pour into a 9 x 13-inch (23 x 33-cm) pan. Add the seitan slices. Cover and marinate in the refrigerator for 1 hour or longer.

When ready to prepare the sandwiches, heat a grill pan over medium-high heat. Drain the seitan, reserving the marinade. Set aside 3 tablespoons (45 ml) marinade in a small bowl. Spray the grill with nonstick spray. Grill the seitan, basting with the rest of the marinade, for 5 minutes, or until marked. Turn and cook the other side for 3 minutes, or until marked.

**TO ASSEMBLE THE SANDWICHES:** Heat the oil in a large skillet over medium heat. Add the onion, cumin, and garlic. Cook for 2 to 3 minutes, or until fragrant. Add the beans and reserved 3 tablespoons (45 ml) marinade. Increase the heat to high and cook for 3 minutes, stirring often. Smash the beans with a fork until you have the consistency of refried beans. Taste and adjust the seasonings with salt and pepper. Divide the beans among the bottoms of the buns. Layer with the seitan. Spread 1 tablespoon (14 g) mayonnaise on the top of each bun. Place on the sandwich and serve.

### SERVING SUGGESTIONS AND VARIATIONS

Add some papaya slices, slivered green bell pepper, and arugula to the sandwiches.

# CHAZWICH

Celine's husband, Chaz, gave us the super-important mission of re-creating a sandwich he enjoyed at a local deli, which surprised us because he usually is no big fan of zucchini. We complied, and here's our take on it. Oh, and yes, he loved our version even more than the original, without threats of having to sleep on the couch if he said otherwise.

**YIELD**
4 SANDWICHES
1 SCANT CUP (215 G) SPREAD

**FOR SPICY SPREAD**

6 ounces (170 g) drained firm silken tofu

2 tablespoons (30 ml) olive oil

1 tablespoon (15 ml) fresh lime juice

½ teaspoon fine sea salt, to taste

Black pepper, to taste

¼ to ½ teaspoon cayenne pepper, to taste

½ teaspoon onion powder

**FOR SANDWICHES**

1½ teaspoons olive oil

1½ teaspoons apple cider vinegar

Salt and pepper, to taste

5 ounces (150 g) zucchini (about 1 medium), trimmed and cut lengthwise into ⅓-inch (8-mm) slices

Four 4 x 3-inch (10 x 8-cm) panini rolls, lightly toasted and rubbed with a garlic clove

8 small heart of romaine lettuce leaves

4 roasted red bell pepper halves, thoroughly drained and lightly squeezed to remove extra moisture

4 marinated artichoke hearts, thoroughly drained and lightly squeezed to remove extra moisture

**TO MAKE THE SPREAD:** Combine all the ingredients in a food processor and process until smooth, scraping the sides with a rubber spatula as needed. Store in an airtight container in the fridge for up to 1 week.

**TO ASSEMBLE THE SANDWICHES:** Combine the olive oil, vinegar, salt, and pepper in a medium-size bowl. Brush the zucchini slices with the dressing. Place the zucchini on a hot grill or grill pan and cook for about 4 minutes per side, until grill marks appear and the slices are tender.

Smear a heaping tablespoon (20 g) spread on each half of the rolls. Divide the zucchini slices equally among the sandwiches, then top each with 2 lettuce leaves, 1 bell pepper half, and 1 artichoke heart. Replace the top halves of the rolls and serve.

# ETHIOPIAN WRAPS

Cool, lemony mint potato salad is combined with hot and spicy stew, all topped with a fresh tomato salad in this easy wrap. Don't be fooled by the ingredient list. It really is a cinch to make!

| | YIELD |
|---|---|
| | 4 WRAPS |

## FOR POTATO SALAD

1 package (1 pound, or 454 g) frozen hash browns, prepared

2 tablespoons (30 ml) fresh lemon juice

½ teaspoon minced fresh mint

Salt and pepper, to taste

## FOR STEW AND WRAPS

1 can (15 ounces, or 425 g) chickpeas, drained and rinsed

1 teaspoon olive oil

½ teaspoon paprika

1 tablespoon (14 g) nondairy butter

½ cup (80 g) minced red onion

½ to 1 teaspoon berbere spice, to taste (see Note)

1 cup (90 g) chopped green cabbage

¼ cup (33 g) minced carrot

1½ teaspoons grated ginger

3 cloves garlic, minced

⅓ cup (80 ml) dry red wine, or more if needed

2 tablespoons (33 g) tomato paste

Salt and pepper, to taste

Four 10-inch (25 cm) flour tortillas

## FOR TOMATO SALAD

1 large tomato, seeded and chopped

½ cup (70 g) diced cucumber

3 tablespoons (30 g) minced red onion

1 tablespoon (9 g) minced jalapeño pepper

2 teaspoons seasoned rice vinegar

Salt and pepper, to taste

**TO MAKE THE POTATO SALAD:** Crumble the cooked hash browns into a medium-size bowl. Add the lemon juice, mint, salt, and pepper. Gently mix. Cover and chill in the refrigerator while you make the stew.

**TO MAKE THE STEW:** Preheat the oven to 400°F (200°C, or gas mark 6). In a 9 x 13-inch (23 x 33-cm) pan, combine the chickpeas, oil, and paprika. Stir to coat. Bake for 12 to 14 minutes, or until the chickpeas start to look dry. Remove from the oven and set aside.

Melt the butter in a large skillet over medium heat. Add the onion and cook for 5 minutes. Add the chickpeas, berbere spice, cabbage, carrot, ginger, garlic, wine, and tomato paste. Simmer for 5 minutes, adding 1 tablespoon (15 ml) more wine if needed to keep moist. The mixture should be thick but not dry. Season to taste with salt and pepper.

**TO MAKE THE TOMATO SALAD:** Combine all the ingredients in a small bowl.

**TO ASSEMBLE THE WRAPS:** Spread ½ cup (77 g) potato salad in the center of each wrap. Top with ½ cup (91 g) chickpea stew and a heaping ¼ cup (42 g) tomato salad. Fold the ends in, roll up, serve.

### RECIPE NOTE

Berbere spice can be found in the ethnic aisle of well-stocked grocery stores. It is a blend of spices popular in Ethiopian cooking. Different brands vary in heat, so be sure to season to taste.

# SCRAMBLED BURRITOS

These protein-filled, stick-to-the-ribs, crispy burritos are mild enough to be enjoyed for breakfast or brunch, especially when served without the optional hot sauce. That is, unless you don't mind having your taste buds awoken rather unceremoniously.

**YIELD**
8 BURRITOS

1½ cups (355 ml) coconut milk or unsweetened plain nondairy milk

2½ cups (600 g) canned diced tomatoes, undrained

½ cup (60 g) nutritional yeast

¼ cup (15 g) chopped fresh parsley

¼ cup (4 g) chopped fresh cilantro

1 teaspoon smoked sea salt, to taste

½ teaspoon ground black pepper, to taste

1 teaspoon smoked paprika

1 teaspoon dried basil

1 tablespoon (15 ml) olive oil

¾ cup (75 g) chopped scallion

8 ounces (227 g) tempeh, cut into ⅓-inch (8-mm) cubes

1 can (15 ounces, or 425 g) cannellini or black beans, drained and rinsed

2 tablespoons (33 g) tomato paste

4 to 6 cloves garlic, minced, to taste

2 to 4 tablespoons (15 to 30 g) corn flour, as needed

Eight 9-inch (23 cm) flour tortillas

Nonstick cooking spray

Hot sauce, for serving (optional)

Combine the milk, tomatoes, nutritional yeast, parsley, cilantro, salt, pepper, paprika, and basil in a large bowl. Set aside.

Heat the oil in a large skillet, add the scallion and tempeh cubes, and sauté over medium-high heat for about 6 minutes, stirring often, until the tempeh is golden brown. Add a little salt if desired and the beans, tomato paste, and garlic, and cook for 1 minute longer. Add the milk mixture and simmer for 10 minutes, or until thickened. Sprinkle 2 tablespoons (15 g) of the corn flour on top and stir it in, cooking to thicken. Add the remaining 1 to 2 tablespoons (8 to 15 g) corn flour if the sauce is still too soupy: you want it to be thick enough to fit in a flour tortilla without making it soggy, but the tempeh preparation should not be too dry either.

Spread ½ cup (150 g) tempeh filling in the bottom center of the tortilla. Fold the bottom and sides of the tortilla over the filling, leaving the top open; it is easier than slicing the burritos in half later and it allows you to be a little more generous with the filling, which will be thick enough not to escape as the burrito is cooked.

Heat a large skillet over medium-low heat. Move it away from the stove once it's warm, carefully coat it with spray, and cook the burritos, seam side down, until golden brown and crispy and the filling is heated through, about 5 minutes on each side. Drizzle with the hot sauce upon serving.

**SERVING SUGGESTIONS AND VARIATIONS**

If you don't want to use tempeh, add an extra can (15 ounces, or 425 g) cannellini or black beans instead, making sure you rinse and drain the beans. Sauté the scallions until they are tender, about 2 minutes, add the beans, then the tomato paste, and then continue with the recipe.

# TASTE OF TUSCANY

Garlic toasted bread gives these sandwiches a savory crunch. Feel free to add some Mushroom Tomato Slices (page 183) or Gobbler Slices (page 182) to make the sandwich a little heartier.

**YIELD**
4 SANDWICHES

**FOR ROASTED TOMATOES**

8 Roma tomatoes, quartered and seeded

1 tablespoon (15 ml) olive oil

1 teaspoon dried Italian seasoning blend

3 large cloves garlic, thickly sliced

Generous pinches of salt and pepper

**FOR SPREAD**

¼ cup plus 2 tablespoons (84 g) vegan mayonnaise

Reserved roasted garlic from tomatoes (above)

2 tablespoons (13 g) minced kalamata olives

2 tablespoons (13 g) minced green olives

2 teaspoons drained capers

Black pepper, to taste

**FOR SANDWICHES**

¼ cup (56 g) nondairy butter, softened

¾ teaspoon garlic salt

8 slices Italian bread

1 cup (30 g) baby spinach

1 green bell pepper, cored and cut into thin strips

4 thin slices red onion, separated into rings

Handful fresh basil leaves

**TO MAKE THE ROASTED TOMATOES:** Preheat the oven to 450°F (230°C, or gas mark 8). Combine all the ingredients on a large rimmed baking sheet. Roast for 15 minutes, or until the tomatoes have a few charred spots. Remove from the oven, let cool, and slip off the tomato skins.

**TO MAKE THE SPREAD:** Combine the mayonnaise and the garlic in a small blender. Blend until smooth. Stir in the remaining ingredients.

**TO ASSEMBLE THE SANDWICHES:** Preheat a panini press fitted with smooth plates on high. Mix the butter and garlic salt together in a small bowl. Spread the outside of the bread slices with the garlic butter. Divide the mayonnaise spread evenly on the inside of the slices. Layer on the spinach, roasted tomatoes, bell pepper, onion, and basil leaves and top with the remaining bread slices, buttered sides out. Grill with the press open for 2 to 3 minutes, or until golden. Turn and cook the other side for 2 to 3 minutes. Cut in half on the diagonal and serve.

# APPLE TEMPEH TRIANGLE DIPPERS

These turnover-like triangle dippers can be served any time of day, at any temperature.

**YIELD**
16 TRIANGLES, OR 4 SERVINGS

### FOR TRIANGLES

Nonstick cooking spray

1 cup (150 g) peeled, cored, and diced crisp apple

¾ cup (94 g) cooked, diced tempeh bacon, homemade (page 179) or store-bought

¼ cup (45 g) pomegranate seeds

1 tablespoon (15 ml) fresh lemon juice

Pinch of ground cinnamon

All-purpose flour, for dusting

2 sheets vegan puff pastry, thawed as per directions

### FOR POMEGRANATE-MAPLE DIPPING SAUCE

¾ cup (180 ml) pomegranate juice, divided

2 tablespoons (30 ml) pure maple syrup

1 tablespoon (15 ml) fresh lemon juice

1 tablespoon (8 g) cornstarch

**TO MAKE THE TRIANGLES:** Preheat the oven to 400°F (200°C, or gas mark 6). Lightly spray two baking sheets with nonstick spray. In a medium-size bowl, combine the apple, tempeh, pomegranate seeds, lemon juice, and cinnamon.

On a lightly floured surface, roll 1 pastry sheet into a 12 x 12-inch (30 x 30-cm) square. Cut into 4 equal squares, then cut the squares on the diagonal to form 8 triangles. Repeat with the remaining sheet puff pastry. Place 1 tablespoon (11 g) filling in each triangle. Be sure to get apple, seeds, and tempeh in each for a balance of flavor and texture. Fold the triangles closed, pressing the seams with your fingers. Repeat with the remaining triangles and filling. Place on the baking sheets and bake for 15 minutes, or until golden. While they are baking, make the sauce. To enjoy later, place the cooked triangles on a wire rack to cool.

**TO MAKE THE SAUCE:** Heat ½ cup (120 ml) of the juice, the maple syrup, and the lemon juice in a small saucepan over medium-high heat. In a small bowl, whisk together the remaining ¼ cup (60 ml) juice and the cornstarch. When the mixture is boiling, add the cornstarch slurry and whisk constantly until the sauce thickens, 3 to 4 minutes. It should be a syrupy consistency. Remove from the heat and divide among 4 bowls for serving. To enjoy later, store the sauce in an airtight container.

**TO SERVE:** Place 4 triangles on each of 4 plates and dip the triangles into the sauce.

### SERVING SUGGESTIONS AND VARIATIONS

Instead of pomegranate-maple dipping sauce, make mustard-maple sauce. In a small bowl, combine 2 tablespoons (30 g) Dijon mustard, 2 tablespoons (30 ml) vegetable broth, and 2 teaspoons pure maple syrup. Mix together well.

# GREEN MONSTER IN THE GARDEN

Quick! Name a vegetable! Is it in here? We couldn't pack them all in, but we tried. The richly flavored tofu provides a perfect base for the crunchy vegetables, giving this sandwich an extra-fresh taste.

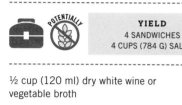

**YIELD**
4 SANDWICHES
4 CUPS (784 G) SALAD

½ cup (120 ml) dry white wine or vegetable broth

1 tablespoon (8 g) nutritional yeast

½ teaspoon lemon pepper

½ teaspoon onion powder

½ teaspoon fine sea salt

¼ teaspoon dried thyme

1 pound (454 g) extra-firm tofu, drained, pressed, and cut into ¼-inch (6-mm) cubes

1 tablespoon (15 ml) olive oil

1 cup (90 g) chopped green cabbage

½ cup (80 g) minced onion

¼ cup (38 g) minced green bell pepper

¼ cup (32 g) minced carrot

¼ cup (29 g) minced radish

¼ cup (30 g) minced celery

¼ cup (60 g) minced dill pickles

2 tablespoons (8 g) minced fresh parsley

½ cup (112 g) vegan mayonnaise

1 tablespoon (15 g) mustard

1 tablespoon (15 ml) apple cider vinegar

Fine sea salt and pepper, to taste

3 tablespoons (42 g) nondairy butter

8 slices Green Monster Bread (page 178) or sandwich bread of choice

1 large tomato, sliced

In a small bowl, mix together the wine, nutritional yeast, lemon pepper, onion powder, salt, and thyme. Heat a large skillet over medium heat. Add the tofu and the wine mixture. Cook, stirring, until the liquid has been absorbed, about 12 minutes. Add the oil and continue to cook until the tofu is golden, about 4 minutes longer. Remove from the skillet, transfer to a medium-size bowl, and let cool.

Add the cabbage, onion, bell pepper, carrot, radish, celery, pickles, parsley, mayonnaise, mustard, and vinegar to the tofu. Stir to combine. Season to taste with salt and pepper. Refrigerate in an airtight container until ready to use. You will have some salad left over; save for another use.

Preheat a panini press fitted with the smooth plates on high. Spread butter on one side of each bread slice. Place ¾ cup (147 g) salad on the unbuttered sides of 4 slices of bread. Top with the tomato slices and the second slices of bread with the buttered sides out. Grill the sandwiches with the press open for 3 minutes, or until golden brown. Turn and grill the other side for 3 minutes, or until golden. Cut in half and serve.

**SERVING SUGGESTIONS AND VARIATIONS**

• We really like the texture that toasting the sandwich brings forward, but this also makes a terrific picnic sandwich on untoasted bread. For packing it untoasted, we suggest adding the tomato right before eating.

• It's also delicious as a lettuce wrap, even if it is a bit messy.

# MEDITERRANEAN TEMPEH SANDWICHES

We've got a little trick to share with you: tempeh, while still warm, absorbs more flavor than when it's cold. That's what we do here. Give it a try. Like the Green Monster in the Garden on the previous page, this is an especially easy-to-pack sandwich if made as a cold sandwich or a wrap.

**YIELD**
4 SANDWICHES

### FOR TEMPEH SALAD

8 ounces (227 g) tempeh

½ teaspoon onion powder

¼ teaspoon black pepper

¼ teaspoon garlic powder

¼ teaspoon turmeric

1 tablespoon (15 ml) canola oil

¼ cup (40 g) minced onion

¼ cup (38 g) minced green bell pepper

2 tablespoons (7 g) minced sun-dried toma-toes (moist vacuum-packed, not oil-packed)

1 artichoke heart, patted dry and minced

1 tablespoon (15 g) minced celery

1 tablespoon (6 g) minced black olive

1 tablespoon (9 g) minced pepperoncini

1 tablespoon (3 g) minced fresh basil

1 tablespoon (4 g) minced fresh parsley

⅓ cup (75 g) vegan mayonnaise

2 teaspoons fresh lemon juice

2 teaspoons white wine vinegar

1 clove garlic, minced

### FOR SANDWICHES

2 tablespoons (28 g) nondairy butter

8 slices Green Monster Bread (page 178) or other sandwich bread

1 cup (30 g) baby spinach

**TO MAKE THE TEMPEH SALAD:** Fill a large skillet three-quarters of the way with water. Bring to a boil over high heat. Place the tempeh in the water, reduce the heat to a simmer, and cook for 20 minutes. In a medium-size bowl, combine the onion powder, pepper, garlic powder, and turmeric.

Drain the tempeh and cut into ¼-inch (6-mm) cubes. While still warm, coat the tempeh with the spice mixture. Heat the oil in a large skillet over medium-high heat. Add the tempeh and cook for 5 minutes, stirring, until golden.

Put the tempeh back into the spice mix. Add the onion, bell pepper, sun-dried tomatoes, artichoke heart, celery, olive, pepperoncini, basil, and parsley. Stir to combine. Add the mayonnaise, lemon juice, vinegar, and garlic. Stir well and adjust the seasonings. Refrigerate in an airtight container until ready to use.

**TO ASSEMBLE THE SANDWICHES:** Preheat a panini press on high. Butter one side of each bread slice. Place ¼ cup (8 g) spinach on 4 of the unbuttered slices. Top with ¾ cup (128 g) tempeh salad and another slice of bread with the buttered side out. Place in the press, close the press, and grill for 8 to 10 minutes, or until golden. Cut in half on the diagonal and serve.

# CHAPTER SEVEN

## SWEETNESS FOLLOWS

{ **SWEET DESSERTS FOR A PERFECTLY SANDWICHED FINAL TOUCH TO YOUR MEAL** }

In a perfect world, dessert wouldn't be merely optional, but an actual requirement to punctuate every meal. We're sure you'll agree that it's hard to have a grumpy face when your hands and mouth are full of all sorts of cookie sandwiches and whoopie pies. Somehow, sandwiched desserts feel extra indulgent, thanks to the doubled sides. Pack a little sweetness into your life—you'll be glad you did.

# SESAME BERRY ICE CREAM SANDWICHES

A pair of surprisingly caramel-like cookies surrounds a delicately flavored, pink-hued frozen concoction that will put all the other ice cream sandwiches you've ever had to shame. Or your money back. (Not really.)

## FOR ICE CREAM

1 cup (235 ml) full-fat coconut milk

8 ounces (227 g) drained firm silken tofu

¾ cup (252 g) agave nectar

1 heaping cup (250 g) frozen raspberries, thawed

1 tablespoon (15 ml) rose water

1 teaspoon pure vanilla extract

## FOR COOKIES

¾ cup (192 g) tahini

⅓ cup (105 g) agave nectar

½ cup (110 g) packed light brown sugar

2 teaspoons pure vanilla extract

1 cup (125 g) all-purpose flour

3 tablespoons (24 g) sesame seeds

¼ teaspoon baking powder

½ teaspoon fine sea salt

Unsweetened plain nondairy milk, as needed

**TO MAKE THE ICE CREAM:** Freeze the tub of your ice cream maker for at least 24 hours. Place all the ingredients in a blender and blend until perfectly smooth. Transfer to the frozen tub. Following the manufacturer's instructions, prepare the ice cream until it is firm. Place in the freezer until ready to use, to firm up even more.

**TO MAKE THE COOKIES:** Preheat the oven to 325°F (170°C, or gas mark 3). Line two cookie sheets with silicone baking mats or parchment paper.

In a large bowl, combine the tahini, agave nectar, sugar, and vanilla. Combine the flour, sesame seeds, baking powder, and salt in another bowl. Add on top of the wet ingredients, and stir until combined. The texture of the dough will vary depending on the thickness of the tahini, so if it is too dry, add just enough nondairy milk for the dough to be manageable and not crumbly.

Scoop out 2 tablespoons (50 g) dough per cookie and flatten slightly. Repeat to make 12 cookies. The cookies won't spread too much, but there won't be enough room for all of them on a single sheet. Place 6 cookies per sheet.

Bake for 12 to 14 minutes, or until golden brown. Let cool on the sheet for a couple of minutes before transferring to a wire rack to cool completely. Place the cookies in the freezer for 1 hour before sandwiching with the ice cream.

**TO ASSEMBLE THE SANDWICHES:** Let the ice cream sit at room temperature for about 15 minutes to soften. Place about 2 tablespoons (30 ml) ice cream between 2 cookies and squeeze lightly to spread the ice cream to the edges. Wrap tightly in plastic and place the sandwiches on a plate. Place in the freezer for 30 minutes so the ice cream can firm up again before enjoying.

# FRUIT ROLL-UPS

We figured it would be good to feature a rather healthy, yet satisfying dessert among all the decadence. This one has a clear enough conscience that it could fit on the breakfast menu without missing a beat. It would be great served after a light salad-type lunch, or maybe even as lunch on its own, especially when you're feeling pressed for time but need something to take the edge off both your hunger and your sweet tooth.

**YIELD**
4 ROLL-UPS

**FOR SPREAD**

¼ cup (64 g) unsweetened creamy peanut butter

Pinch of salt, if the peanut butter is unsalted

¼ cup (60 g) pumpkin purée (not pie filling)

½ teaspoon ground cinnamon or pumpkin pie spice

½ teaspoon pure vanilla extract

2 tablespoons (30 ml) pure maple syrup or (42 g) agave nectar

**FOR ROLL-UPS**

Four 8-inch (20 cm) flour tortillas

¼ cup (41 g) packed raisins, dried cherries, or dried cranberries

2 firm ripe bananas, peeled and cut in half lengthwise

1 recipe vanilla dipping sauce (page 30) or 2 containers (6 ounces, or 170 g each) vanilla-flavored nondairy yogurt (optional)

**TO MAKE THE SPREAD:** Combine all the ingredients in a medium-size bowl.

**TO ASSEMBLE THE ROLL-UPS:** Smear 2 generous tablespoons (46 g) spread in the center of each tortilla, leaving a 1-inch (2.5-cm) margin all around. Sprinkle 1 tablespoon (10 g) raisins in a line on the right side of the tortilla (place them on the spread so that it acts like glue) and place ½ banana on top. Roll the tortillas up into a tight cigar, and dip into the sauce.

**SERVING SUGGESTIONS AND VARIATIONS**

Use different fruits depending on what is in season (apples, pears, peaches) and add a handful of nuts for extra crunch.

# CHOCOLATE ALMOND GELATO–FILLED MINI BRIOCHES

If you thought there was no way of making vegan brioche even better, try this: put a big scoop of luscious, rich, and creamy gelato in a miniature brioche, drizzle with chocolate syrup, and be a happy foodie camper.

## FOR GELATO

1⅓ cups (315 ml) unsweetened almond milk, divided

⅓ to ½ cup (60 to 100 g) sugar, to taste

¼ cup (20 g) unsweetened cocoa powder

¼ cup (64 g) toasted almond butter

1 teaspoon pure vanilla extract

Generous ¼ teaspoon pure almond extract (optional)

Pinch of fine sea salt

## FOR BRIOCHES

Nonstick cooking spray

1 recipe brioche dough (page 177), prepared to after refrigeration

Vegan chocolate syrup, for serving (optional)

**TO MAKE THE GELATO:** Freeze the tub of your ice cream maker for at least 24 hours. Combine all the ingredients in a blender, blending until perfectly smooth. Following the manufacturer's instructions, prepare the ice cream until it is firm. You might have to place it in the freezer for a couple of hours, to get a firmer texture.

**TO MAKE THE BRIOCHES:** Lightly coat eight 3½-inch (9-cm) mini brioche pans with nonstick spray. Divide the dough into 8 portions, shape each into a round, and place in the pans. Slightly moisten your hands and smooth the tops, if needed. Loosely cover with plastic wrap and let rise for 1 to 1½ hours, until doubled.

Preheat the oven to 400°F (200°C, or gas mark 6). Carefully remove the plastic wrap and bake the mini brioches for 10 minutes. Lower the temperature to 350°F (180°C, or gas mark 4) and bake the brioches for 6 minutes longer, or until their tops are a deep golden brown color. Carefully remove them from the pans and transfer to a wire rack to cool.

**TO ASSEMBLE THE BRIOCHES:** Let the ice cream sit at room temperature for about 15 minutes to soften. Using a sharp knife, dig a cone out of the top of each brioche, large enough to fit a small scoop of gelato. Cut out the pointy end of the brioche cone so that the top hat is flat. Place a small scoop of gelato inside, and top with the brioche hat. Drizzle with the chocolate syrup and serve immediately.

# MANGO BUTTER & GINGER WHOOPIE PIES

We love the chocolate and cream whoopie pie combo as much as the next person, but how about trying something a little more titillating and unusual this time? These are perfect for autumn, but we're so hooked on them we make them year-round.

| **YIELD** |
| :---: |
| 8 WHOOPIE PIES |

### FOR MANGO BUTTER

2 cups (280 g) frozen mango chunks

2 tablespoons (30 ml) water

1 tablespoon (15 ml) fresh lemon juice

¼ cup (55 g) packed light brown sugar

### FOR COOKIES

⅓ cup (75 g) nondairy butter, at room temperature

¾ cup (165 g) packed light brown sugar

¾ cup (216 g) Mango Butter

2 tablespoons (16 g) cornstarch

1½ teaspoons ground ginger

½ teaspoon fine sea salt

2¼ cups (281 g) all-purpose flour

1 teaspoon baking powder

½ teaspoon baking soda

### FOR FROSTING

2 tablespoons (24 g) vegan shortening

2 tablespoons (28 g) nondairy butter

¼ teaspoon ground ginger

1½ cups (180 g) powdered sugar, sifted

1 tablespoon (15 ml) nondairy milk

½ teaspoon pure vanilla extract

**TO MAKE THE MANGO BUTTER:** Combine all ingredients in a medium-size saucepan. Bring to a boil, then lower the heat to medium and cook for 8 minutes, until the mango is tender enough to mash. Transfer to a blender (use caution when blending hot foods!) and blend until perfectly smooth. Let cool completely.

**TO MAKE THE COOKIES:** With an electric mixer, beat the butter and sugar until fluffy. Add the mango butter, cornstarch, ginger, and salt and beat until combined. Sift and combine the flour, baking powder, and baking soda in another bowl. Add on top of the wet ingredients, and beat until just combined. The dough should be fluffy, but thick enough to be held in your hand.

Preheat the oven to 350°F (180°C, or gas mark 4). Line two baking sheets with parchment paper.

Scoop out 2 tablespoons (45 g) dough per cookie. Roll it between your hands and flatten slightly. Place 2 inches (5 cm) apart on the cookie sheets. Repeat to make 16 cookies. Bake for 12 minutes, or until set. Cool on a wire rack.

**TO MAKE THE FROSTING:** Cream the shortening and butter with an electric mixer until smooth. Add the ginger and sugar. Mix on low speed, then beat until combined. Add the milk and vanilla. Mix on low speed until combined, then beat on medium speed for 2 minutes until fluffy, occasionally stopping to scrape the sides of the bowl with a rubber spatula.

**TO ASSEMBLE THE WHOOPIE PIES:** Spread 1 generous tablespoon (30 g) frosting on the bottom of one cookie and top with another cookie, pressing down gently to spread the frosting.

# BANANAS FOSTER CAKE SANDWICHES

Back in their nonvegan days, Celine and her husband used to go to chain restaurants that shall remain nameless, and poke fun at the over-the-top dessert menus. They clearly had too much time on their hands and now sheepishly admit that those restaurants may have been on to something: over-the-top can be a good thing, as this particular treat proudly demonstrates.

| YIELD |
| --- |
| 8 SANDWICHES, 12 OUNCES (355 ML) ICE CREAM |
| ¾ CUP (180 ML) CARAMEL |

**FOR ICE CREAM**

1 recipe vanilla dipping sauce (page 30)

**FOR CAKES**

Nonstick cooking spray

1 heaping cup (240 g) mashed ripe bananas

Scant ⅔ cup (120 g) granulated sugar

⅓ cup (80 ml) light olive oil

1 tablespoon (8 g) arrowroot powder

1 teaspoon pure vanilla extract

1½ cups (188 g) all-purpose flour

2 teaspoons baking powder

½ teaspoon fine sea salt

**FOR CARAMEL**

2 tablespoons (28 g) nondairy butter

½ cup (110 g) packed brown sugar

Pinch of fine sea salt

1 tablespoon (15 ml) dark rum

¼ cup plus 1 tablespoon (75 ml) unsweetened plain nondairy creamer, divided

2 teaspoons cornstarch

**TO MAKE THE ICE CREAM:** Freeze the tub of your ice cream maker for at least 24 hours. Place the vanilla sauce in the frozen tub. Following the manufacturer's instructions, prepare the ice cream until it is firm. Place ice cream in the freezer while preparing the cakes and caramel.

**TO MAKE THE CAKES:** Preheat the oven to 350°F (180°C, or gas mark 4). Lightly coat two 5¾ x 3-inch (14 x 8-cm) loaf pans with spray.

Combine the bananas, sugar, oil, arrowroot, and vanilla in a large bowl. Sift and combine the flour, baking powder, and salt in another bowl. Add on top of the wet ingredients, and stir until just combined. Divide between the prepared pans. Bake for 35 minutes, or until a toothpick inserted into the middle comes out clean. Carefully remove the loaves from the pans and let cool completely on a wire rack.

**TO MAKE THE CARAMEL:** Combine the butter, sugar, salt, rum, and ¼ cup (60 ml) creamer in a medium-size saucepan and cook over medium-high heat until the sugar dissolves, about 3 minutes. Combine the remaining 1 tablespoon (15 ml) creamer with the cornstarch, stirring to form a paste. Add the paste to the syrup and cook just until slightly thickened, about 1 minute. Remove from the heat and keep warm.

When ready to assemble, let the ice cream sit at room temperature for about 15 minutes to soften. Cut both mini loaves into 8 slices. Place a mini-scoop (about 3 tablespoons [45 ml]) ice cream on top. Drizzle warm caramel sauce over all. Top with another slice of cake. If you prefer, serve open-faced and double the ice cream and caramel fun.

# GINGER CREAM CRÊPES WITH PEARS

We occasionally deem it perfectly acceptable to prepare this elegant dessert for breakfast because it's made of yogurt and fruit—and crêpes are just a thinner form of pancakes, after all. Denial is a great thing.

### FOR ICE CREAM

1¼ cups (300 g) unsweetened plain nondairy yogurt

¾ cup (180 g) nondairy cream cheese

⅓ cup (67 g) sugar

1 tablespoon (5 g) ground ginger, to taste

### FOR PEARS

2 tablespoons (30 ml) thawed apple juice concentrate

2 large firm pears, cored and diced

2 tablespoons (28 g) packed light brown sugar

### FOR CRÊPES

2 tablespoons (28 g) nondairy butter, melted

1½ tablespoons (12 g) cornstarch

1 cup (235 ml) unsweetened plain nondairy milk

1 teaspoon pure vanilla extract

Pinch of fine sea salt

2 tablespoons (25 g) sugar

½ cup (63 g) all-purpose flour

1 tablespoon (8 g) chickpea flour

Nonstick cooking spray

**TO MAKE THE ICE CREAM:** Freeze the tub of your ice cream maker for at least 24 hours. Blend the yogurt, cream cheese, sugar, and ginger in a food processor, stopping to scrape the sides occasionally, until perfectly smooth. Transfer to the frozen tub. Following the manufacturer's instructions, prepare the ice cream until it is firm. Place ice cream in the freezser while preparing the rest of the recipe.

**TO MAKE THE PEARS:** Combine the juice and pears in a small saucepan over medium heat. Cook for 4 minutes, or until the pears are just tender but not mushy. Add the sugar and cook until dissolved and caramelized, about 2 minutes. Set aside.

**TO MAKE THE CRÊPES:** In a large bowl, whisk the melted butter with the cornstarch until dissolved. Add the milk, vanilla, salt, and sugar. Sift the flours on top, and whisk until completely smooth.

Heat a 10-inch (25-cm) nonstick skillet over medium-high heat, move it away from the stove once it's warm, and carefully coat it with spray. Place it back on the stove and add ⅓ cup (80 ml) batter, tilting the pan so that the batter thins out and covers about 7 inches (18 cm) of the pan. Cook until the edges and surface are light golden brown, 3 to 5 minutes. Flip and cook for 1 to 3 minutes longer, until light golden brown. Transfer to a plate. Repeat with the remaining batter to make 3 more crêpes.

**TO ASSEMBLE THE WRAPS:** Let the ice cream sit at room temperature for about 15 minutes to soften. Place 1 crêpe on a plate. Place 1 to 2 small scoops of ice cream in the center of the crêpe. Fold the sides of the crêpe over the ice cream. Divide the diced pears equally among the crêpes, placing them on top or on the side. Serve immediately.

# PEANUT BUTTER BROWNIE SANDWICHES

One of our testers made a batch of these for her Labor Day celebration, and she told us that of all the desserts that were offered that day, these were the clear winners. It really is impossible not to have the upper hand when peanut butter and chocolate are involved. Unless you don't like peanut butter and chocolate, that is. And yes, we are gloating.

**YIELD**
7 SANDWICHES

### FOR BROWNIES

⅔ cup (150 g) nondairy butter

1 cup (220 g) packed brown sugar

2 teaspoons pure vanilla extract

¼ cup (60 g) plain or vanilla-flavored nondairy yogurt

1½ cups (188 g) all-purpose flour

½ cup (40 g) unsweetened cocoa powder

½ teaspoon baking powder

½ teaspoon fine sea salt

### FOR FROSTING

½ cup (128 g) creamy salted unsweetened peanut butter

3 tablespoons (36 g) vegan shortening

⅓ cup (40 g) powdered sugar, sifted

½ teaspoon pure vanilla extract

**TO MAKE THE BROWNIES:** Preheat the oven to 350°F (180°C, or gas mark 4). Line two baking sheets with parchment paper or silicone baking mats.

Using an electric mixer, cream the butter, sugar, vanilla, and yogurt until smooth. Sift and combine the flour, cocoa, baking powder, and salt in another bowl. Add them on top of the wet ingredients and beat until just combined. The batter will be soft and almost cakelike. Scoop 2 tablespoons (50 g) dough per cookie onto the baking sheet, leaving approximately 2 inches (5 cm) between cookies. Flatten the cookies slightly. Repeat to make 14 cookies. Bake for 14 to 16 minutes (the cookies should look dry on the surface) and remove from the oven. Carefully transfer the cookies to a cooling rack. Let cool completely before assembling.

**TO MAKE THE FROSTING:** Using an electric mixer, cream the peanut butter and shortening until smooth. Add the powdered sugar and vanilla, and beat until fluffy.

**TO ASSEMBLE THE SANDWICHES:** Spread 1 tablespoon (16 g) peanut butter frosting on the bottom of a brownie. Top with the bottom of another brownie. Repeat with the remaining brownies and frosting.

# OREO WAFFLEWICHES

Have you ever bitten into an Oreo cookie feeling that it's too small for your demanding needs? We took matters into our own hands and gave ourselves (and you!) a perfect excuse to have an Oreo cookie, made bigger and "wafflier."

**YIELD**
3 OR 6 WAFFLEWICHES

**FOR WAFFLES**

1 cup (235 ml) plain, vanilla, or chocolate soymilk

⅓ cup (67 g) sugar

¼ cup (56 g) nondairy butter, melted

¼ teaspoon fine sea salt

1 teaspoon pure vanilla extract

1 cup (125 g) all-purpose flour

¼ cup (20 g) Dutch-processed cocoa powder

1 teaspoon baking powder

1½ tablespoons (12 g) cornstarch

Nonstick cooking spray

**FOR FROSTING**

2 tablespoons (24 g) vegan shortening

2 tablespoons (28 g) nondairy butter

1½ cups (180 g) powdered sugar, sifted

1 tablespoon (15 ml) nondairy milk

½ teaspoon pure vanilla extract

**FOR SERVING**

Vegan chocolate syrup (optional)

**TO MAKE THE WAFFLES:** Combine the milk, sugar, melted butter, salt, and vanilla in a large bowl. Combine the flour, cocoa, baking powder, and cornstarch in another bowl. Add on top of the wet ingredients and whisk to combine and eliminate lumps, being careful not to overmix. Cook the waffles according to the waffle iron instructions using non-stick cooking spray. The waffles are ready when they look dry on the surface, which should take approximately 6 minutes. You should get 1½ Belgian-size waffles, or 2 to 3 standard-size waffles.

To get the crispness that Oreo cookies are known for, you will need to toast the waffles in a toaster oven before serving. Be sure to let them cool on a wire rack for about 20 minutes before adding the frosting.

**TO MAKE THE FROSTING:** Cream the shortening and butter with an electric mixer until smooth. Slowly add the sugar. Mix on low speed, then beat until combined. Add the milk and vanilla and beat on low speed until combined, then beat on medium speed for 2 minutes until fluffy, occasionally stopping to scrape the sides of the bowl with a rubber spatula.

**TO ASSEMBLE THE WAFFLEWICHES:** Break the waffles into quarters. Divide the frosting equally between half of the quarters, or adjust the amount to your personal taste. Top with the remaining waffle quarters. Drizzle the chocolate syrup on top before serving.

# CHAPTER EIGHT

## THE BUILDING BLOCKS

{ **A FEW INCREDIBLE AND INDISPENSABLE STAPLE RECIPES** }

We wouldn't leave you without sharing a few favorite recipes that will make your life easier, especially if you aren't a fan of store-bought vegan meats and breads. These are everyday staples in our homes, and they make delicious eats so much quicker. A little prep goes a long way in stocking your fridge or freezer. Also (and you might want to hold on to your seat for this one, too): vegan brioche! Not quite a staple, granted, but it has changed our lives for the better. These are recipes that fit in the "last, but definitely not least" category.

◄ *Cinnamon Swirl Bread,*
page 176

# CINNAMON SWIRL BREAD

What's better than freshly baked bread, you ask? A swirl of sugary cinnamon inside the freshly baked bread in question, we say *(pictured on page 174)*.

*(pictured on page 174)*

**YIELD**
1 LOAF

### FOR DOUGH

3 cups (375 g) all-purpose flour, plus more if needed

¼ cup (36 g) vital wheat gluten

¼ cup (55 g) packed light brown sugar

1 teaspoon fine sea salt

1 cup (235 ml) almond milk, lukewarm

2 tablespoons (30 ml) canola oil

2 teaspoons instant yeast

½ teaspoon canola oil

Nonstick cooking spray

### FOR FILLING

1 tablespoon (8 g) arrowroot powder

1 tablespoon (15 ml) warm water

¼ cup (55 g) packed light brown sugar

1 tablespoon (8 g) ground cinnamon

**TO MAKE THE DOUGH:** In a large mixing bowl, combine the flour, gluten, sugar, and salt. Add the milk and oil and stir to combine. Add the yeast. Using a stand mixer fitted with a dough hook, mix until a dough forms. Add extra flour, 1 tablespoon (8 g) at a time, if needed. Mix for about 6 minutes.

Alternatively, if you don't have a stand mixer, transfer the dough to a lightly floured surface and knead for 8 to 10 minutes, until the dough is smooth and pliable.

Lightly oil a large bowl and place the dough in it. Turn to coat. Cover tightly with plastic wrap and let rise for 60 to 90 minutes, until doubled.

Lightly coat an 8 x 4-inch (20 x 10-cm) loaf pan with spray.

**TO MAKE THE FILLING:** Combine all the ingredients in a small bowl. Note that if the filling is too thick to be spread, you can add just a little extra warm water to it. Don't add too much: it should be thick and spreadable, but not pourable.

Gently punch down the dough. Roll it out into an 8 x 18-inch (20 x 45-cm) rectangle with a rolling pin. Carefully spread the filling all over in a thin layer, leaving less than 1 inch (2.5 cm) around the edges. Tightly roll the dough starting at the short side and place it, seam side down, into the greased pan. Loosely cover with plastic wrap and let rise until the dough only slightly peaks over the top of the pan, between 30 and 60 minutes.

Preheat the oven to 350°F (180°C, or gas mark 4). Place a sheet of foil under the pan just in case the filling should escape, and bake for 30 minutes, or until golden brown and the bottom of the bread sounds hollow when tapped. Remove from the pan and let cool completely before slicing.

# BRIOCHE

This tender bread cannot be kneaded by hand, because it would require extra flour and its buttery flavor would be muted. You could use a food processor (with a dough blade) if you don't have a stand mixer. Do not skip the refrigeration step, because it helps with the brioche's structure.

**YIELD**
1 LOAF

1 tablespoon (8 g) cornstarch

½ cup (120 ml) water, divided

½ cup (120 ml) full-fat coconut milk, at room temperature

3 tablespoons (36 g) sugar

½ teaspoon fine sea salt

2 cups (250 g) all-purpose flour

1 tablespoon (12 g) instant yeast

¼ cup (56 g) cold nondairy butter, cut into small pieces

Nonstick cooking spray

Combine the cornstarch and 2 tablespoons (30 ml) of the water in a deep microwave-safe bowl and stir to dissolve the starch. Add the remaining 6 tablespoons (90 ml) water, stir well, and cook for 1 minute, or until the mixture is slightly gelatinous, thickened, and cloudy. Alternatively, do this on the stove in a small saucepan, until the same results are achieved, 1 to 2 minutes. Let cool completely before using.

Whisk the cornstarch mixture, milk, sugar, and salt in the bowl of a stand mixer fitted with a dough hook.

Add the flour and yeast on top. Mix on medium speed for 2 minutes, starting the countdown and raising the speed to medium-high once the ingredients are beginning to combine.

Slowly add the butter while the mixer is on. Once all the butter is in, mix on medium-high speed for 4 minutes, stopping to push the butter down with a spatula if it sticks to the sides of the bowl. Do not add extra flour; it's normal for the dough to look like batter. Gather it in the center of the bowl with a rubber spatula, tightly cover the bowl with plastic wrap, and let stand for 45 minutes. This time mostly serves to ensure adequate moisture.

Use a rubber spatula to gently deflate the dough, and gather it in the center of the bowl again. Tightly cover with plastic wrap again, and refrigerate for 18 hours.

Coat an 8 x 4-inch (20 x 10-cm) loaf pan with spray. Use a rubber spatula to gently deflate the stiff dough. Place the dough in the pan and smooth the top with lightly moistened hands if needed. Loosely cover with plastic wrap, and let rise for 1½ to 2 hours, until doubled.

Preheat the oven to 400°F (200°C, or gas mark 6). Carefully remove the plastic wrap and bake the brioche for 10 minutes. Lower the temperature to 350°F (180°C, or gas mark 4), and bake for 15 to 20 minutes longer, until it reaches a deep golden brown color on top. Carefully remove from the pan, transfer to a wire rack, and let cool completely.

# GREEN MONSTER BREAD

This is the perfect bread for newbie bread bakers, because it is quite responsive and easy to work with. Feel free to replace up to half of the flour with white whole wheat flour, but keep in mind that the green color might become a bit more subdued if you do. For instructions on how to make this dough into rolls or bagels, see page 20.

**YIELD**
1 LOAF

1 packed cup (40 g) baby arugula or spinach

1 tablespoon (8 g) minced garlic

1¼ cups (295 ml) water, lukewarm

2 tablespoons (30 ml) light olive oil

3½ cups (438 g) all-purpose flour, plus more if needed

2 tablespoons (18 g) vital wheat gluten

2 teaspoons instant yeast

2 tablespoons (25 g) sugar

1 teaspoon fine sea salt

½ teaspoon canola oil

Nonstick cooking spray

Place the arugula, garlic, water, and oil in a blender; blend until smooth. In a large mixing bowl, combine the flour, gluten, yeast, sugar, and salt. Add the wet ingredients to the dry. Using a stand mixer fitted with a dough hook, mix for about 6 minutes, until a dough forms. Add more flour, 1 tablespoon (8 g) at a time while mixing, if needed.

Alternatively, if you don't have a stand mixer, transfer the dough to a lightly floured surface and knead for 8 to 10 minutes, adding 1 tablespoon (8 g) flour at a time if needed, until the dough is smooth and pliable.

Lightly oil a large bowl and place the dough in it. Turn to coat. Cover tightly with plastic wrap and let rise for 60 to 90 minutes, until doubled.

Lightly coat an 8 x 4-inch (20 x 10-cm) loaf pan with spray. Gently punch down the dough and press it down into the pan. Loosely cover with plastic wrap and let rise until the dough reaches 1 inch (2.5 cm) over the top of the pan, between 30 and 60 minutes.

Preheat the oven to 375°F (190°C, or gas mark 5). Carefully remove the plastic wrap and bake for 30 minutes, or until golden brown and the bottom of the bread sounds hollow when tapped. Remove from the pan, transfer to a wire rack, and let cool before slicing.

# TEMPEH BACON

With all the rage about bacon, we knew we had to add a cruelty-free option. After all, this is a sandwich book. Feel free to use this tempeh as an addition to any of our sandwiches, or enjoy it next to your favorite pancakes. The two-step preparation lets you get it from the fridge to the plate in minutes.

**YIELD**
8 OUNCES (227 G)

8 ounces (227 g) tempeh

¾ cup (180 ml) vegetable broth

1 tablespoon (15 ml) pure maple syrup

1 tablespoon (16 g) tomato paste

1 tablespoon (15 ml) apple cider vinegar

1 tablespoon (15 ml) tamari

¾ teaspoon ground cumin

¾ teaspoon ground coriander

½ teaspoon fine sea salt

½ teaspoon onion powder

¼ teaspoon garlic powder

1 tablespoon plus 1 teaspoon (20 ml) liquid smoke, divided

2 tablespoons (30 ml) olive oil

Using a serrated knife, carefully cut the tempeh into ¼-inch (6-mm) strips across the short side. In a 9 x 13-inch (23 x 33-cm) pan, combine the broth, syrup, tomato paste, vinegar, tamari, cumin, coriander, salt, onion powder, garlic powder, and 1 tablespoon (15 ml) of the liquid smoke. Place the tempeh strips in the marinade and turn to coat. The strips will probably be touching, which is fine. Cover with foil and refrigerate overnight.

Preheat the oven to 300°F (150°C, or gas mark 2). Bake the strips in the marinade, uncovered, for 30 minutes. Most of the marinade will either be absorbed or coating the tempeh. Remove from the oven. At this point, the strips may be prepared for serving or stored in the refrigerator for up to 1 week and cooked as needed.

To cook, combine the olive oil and remaining 1 teaspoon (5 ml) liquid smoke in a small bowl. Heat a large skillet over medium heat. Brush both sides of the tempeh strips with the olive oil mixture and, working in batches, cook for 4 minutes, or until browned. Turn and cook the other side for about 3 minutes.

# MOO-FREE SEITAN

Long, slow cooking and cooling in vegetable broth imparts a wonderful depth of flavor to seitan. This has become a go-to among our testers. If soy flour is unavailable, chickpea flour may be used.

**YIELD**
2 POUNDS (908 G)
IF COOKED IN A SLOW COOKER
2½ POUNDS (1.1 KG)
IF COOKED IN THE OVEN

### FOR SEITAN

2 cups (288 g) vital wheat gluten, plus more if needed

3 tablespoons (23 g) soy flour

1 tablespoon (8 g) nutritional yeast

2 teaspoons onion powder

1 teaspoon paprika

1 teaspoon garlic powder

½ teaspoon black pepper

1¼ cups (295 ml) vegetable broth, chilled, plus more if needed

¼ cup (60 ml) tamari

3 tablespoons (45 g) ketchup

2 teaspoons liquid smoke

### FOR COOKING BROTH

4 to 6 cups (940 ml to 1.4 l) vegetable broth, chilled (see Note)

1 tablespoon (15 ml) tamari

1 tablespoon (15 g) ketchup

2 large cloves garlic, sliced

¼ small onion, sliced

Generous pinch of pepper

Nonstick cooking spray

**TO MAKE THE SEITAN:** In a medium-size bowl stir the wheat gluten, flour, nutritional yeast, and spices with a fork. Combine the broth, tamari, ketchup and liquid smoke in a small bowl. Mix the wet ingredients into the dry, using a fork. Add an extra 1 or 2 tablespoons (15 to 30 ml) broth or (9 to 18 g) gluten, if needed, to make a workable dough. Knead by hand for 4 minutes, or until the dough forms a cohesive ball and you can see strands of gluten forming. Form into a ball about 5 inches (13 cm) across.

**TO MAKE THE COOKING BROTH:** Combine the broth, tamari, ketchup, garlic, onion, and pepper in a large bowl.

**TO COOK IN A SLOW COOKER:** Place the seitan in the cooker and pour the broth over the ball. Make sure it is covered completely. Cook on low for 8 hours. Cool in the broth. Cut into four 8-ounce (227-g) portions, or as desired. Seitan is best after it has had a chance to cool completely. Wrap tightly in plastic and store in the fridge for up to 1 week or freeze for up to 3 months.

**TO COOK IN THE OVEN:** Preheat the oven to 300°F (150°C, or gas mark 2). Coat a 2-quart (1.9-l) round covered casserole dish with spray. A larger baking dish may be used, but more broth will be needed. Place the seitan in the dish. Cover with the broth. Place on top of a baking sheet in case of drips. Cover and bake for 3 hours. Cool in the broth and package as above.

### RECIPE NOTE

The amount of broth you need will depend on the cooking method. For the oven method, 4 cups (940 ml) should be enough. For the slow cooker, you'll need enough broth to cover the ball of seitan. If you need more than 6 cups (1.4 l), then double the rest of the seasonings in the cooking liquid as well.

# NO CLUCK CUTLETS

This recipe is cruelty-free and so much better for people and the planet than poultry. Store these in your freezer for quick meals any time.

## FOR CUTLETS

2 cups (288 g) vital wheat gluten, plus more if needed

¼ cup (30 g) nutritional yeast

¼ cup (30 g) chickpea flour

¼ cup (30 g) soy flour

2 cloves garlic, minced

1 teaspoon onion powder

¼ teaspoon white pepper

1¼ cups (295 ml) vegetable broth, chilled, plus more if needed

2 tablespoons (30 ml) dry white wine

1 tablespoon (15 ml) olive oil

1 tablespoon (6 g) vegan chicken-flavored bouillon powder (optional)

## FOR COOKING BROTH

3 cups (705 ml) vegetable broth, chilled

1 teaspoon onion powder

½ teaspoon dried thyme

½ teaspoon mustard powder

½ teaspoon fine sea salt

**TO MAKE THE CUTLETS:** In a large bowl, combine the wheat gluten, nutritional yeast, flours, garlic, onion powder, and white pepper. Stir together. In a medium-size bowl, combine the broth, wine, oil, and bouillon and stir together. Mix the wet ingredients into the dry, using a fork. Add an extra 1 or 2 tablespoons (15 to 30 ml) broth or (9 to 18 g) gluten, if needed, to make a workable dough. Knead by hand for 4 minutes, or until the dough forms a cohesive ball and you can see strands of gluten forming. Divide evenly into 10 balls.

**TO MAKE THE COOKING BROTH:** In a large roasting pan, combine all the ingredients. Preheat the oven to 300°F (150°C, or gas mark 2).

**TO COOK:** Between two pieces of parchment paper and using a rolling pin, roll each ball into a thin cutlet about ¼ inch (6 mm) thick. Pour in the broth in the roasting pan and roll the remaining balls into cutlets. It's fine if they touch or overlap some. Cover the pan tightly with foil and bake for 1 hour. Turn off the heat and leave the cutlets in the oven for 1 hour longer. Remove from the oven and let cool in the broth. Wrap tightly in plastic and store in the fridge for up to 1 week or freeze for up to 3 months.

# GOBBLER SLICES

We know what you're thinking, and you're right. That's exactly what we named these after. Many thanks to cookbook author and host of www.everydaydish.tv Julie Hasson for coming up with the popular steaming technique used here.

½ cup (91 g) cooked navy beans

½ cup (120 ml) dry white wine

½ cup (120 ml) vegetable broth, plus more if needed

2 tablespoons (30 ml) fresh lemon juice

2 tablespoons (30 ml) olive oil

2 teaspoons onion powder

1 teaspoon garlic powder

1 teaspoon dried parsley

¾ teaspoon dried sage

½ teaspoon mustard powder

½ teaspoon dried rosemary

½ teaspoon black pepper

½ teaspoon fine sea salt

¼ teaspoon celery seed

1¼ cups (180 g) vital wheat gluten, plus more if needed

¼ cup (30 g) nutritional yeast

2 tablespoons (15 g) chickpea flour or soy flour

2 tablespoons (24 g) instant tapioca, such as Minute Brand

In a blender, combine the beans, wine, broth, lemon juice, oil, and spices. Blend until smooth.

In a medium-size bowl, combine the wheat gluten, nutritional yeast, flour, and tapioca. Pour the liquid into the dry ingredients and mix with a fork. Add an extra 1 tablespoon (15 ml) broth or (9 g) gluten if needed to make a soft, workable dough. Knead for a few minutes, squeezing to be sure all the ingredients are combined. Transfer to a 12-inch (30.5-cm) piece of foil. Form into a roll about 6 inches (15 cm) long. Roll the foil around the mixture, twisting the ends to enclose.

Prepare a steamer. Steam the roll for 1 hour 15 minutes. Let cool completely before slicing thinly, using a sharp, serrated knife and cutting in a seesaw motion. Wrap tightly in plastic and store in the fridge for up to 1 week or freeze for up to 2 months.

# MUSHROOM TOMATO SLICES

The outstanding flavor and texture of these cold cuts really make them special. Huge thanks to author and blogger Nathan Kozuskanich for allowing us to use the "steam, then bake method" he features on his popular blog, Vegan Dad.

**YIELD**
24 OUNCES (680 G)

½ ounce (14 g) dried porcini mushrooms

1 cup (235 ml) boiling water

Broth, as needed

¼ cup (28 g) sun-dried tomatoes (moist vacuum-packed, not oil-packed)

½ cup (91 g) cooked black-eyed peas

⅓ cup (55 g) chopped red onion

¼ cup (60 g) ketchup

¼ cup (60 ml) tamari

2 tablespoons (30 ml) olive oil

1 tablespoon (15 ml) liquid smoke

2 teaspoons smoked paprika

2 teaspoons onion powder

1 teaspoon ground coriander

1 teaspoon red pepper flakes

1 teaspoon garlic powder

1 teaspoon ground cumin

½ teaspoon white pepper

1¼ cups (180 g) vital wheat gluten, plus more if needed

¼ cup (30 g) nutritional yeast

¼ cup (32 g) soy flour or chickpea flour

2 tablespoons (24 g) instant tapioca, such as Minute Brand

Add the dried porcinis to the water and let soak for 30 minutes. Using a coffee filter, drain the mushrooms, reserving the liquid. You will need ⅔ cup (160 ml) liquid. If you don't have the full ⅔ cup (160 ml), add broth or water to make up the difference. Rinse the mushrooms well to remove any dirt. Combine the mushrooms, sun-dried tomatoes, black-eyed peas, onion, ketchup, tamari, oil, liquid smoke, paprika, onion powder, coriander, red pepper flakes, garlic powder, cumin, and white pepper in a blender. Add the reserved liquid and blend until smooth.

In a medium-size bowl, combine the wheat gluten, nutritional yeast, soy flour, and tapioca. Pour the liquid into the dry ingredients and mix with a fork. Add an extra 1 tablespoon (15 ml) broth or (9 g) gluten if needed to make a soft, workable dough. Knead well, squeezing to be sure all ingredients are combined. Divide the mixture evenly between two 12-inch (30.5-cm) pieces of foil. Form into 2 rolls about 5 inches (13 cm) long. Roll the foil around the mixture, twisting the ends to enclose the mixture.

Prepare a steamer. Steam the rolls for 1 hour 15 minutes.

Preheat the oven to 350°F (180°C, or gas mark 4). Place the steamed rolls on a baking sheet and bake for 45 minutes. Let cool completely before slicing thinly, using a sharp, serrated knife and cutting in a seesaw motion. Wrap tightly in plastic and store in the fridge for up to 1 week or freeze for up to 2 months.

# ACKNOWLEDGMENTS

Many grateful thank-yous to Amanda Waddell, Will Kiester, Karen Levy, and Heather Godin for working hard on making this book sound and look as good as it does.

Huge thank-yous to our rockin' team of testers: Courtney Blair, Kim Carpenter, Monika Soria Caruso, Kelly Cavalier, Michelle Cavigliano, Shannon Davis, Kip Dorrell, Ted Lai, Clea Mahoney, Shelly Mocquet-McDonald, Jen Fish Molica, Monique and Michel Narbel-Gimzia, John Plummer, Constanze Reichardt, Nina Stoma, Vegan Aide, and Liz Wyman.

Tami would like to thank Jim, her best friend, and her wonderful family. Huge thanks to Celine for the stellar sandwich fun, and to everyone, everywhere eating vegan, one meal at a time.

Celine would like to thank her (furry and less furry) family. Extra special thank-yous to the always inspiring Tami for what will forever be known as the super summer of sandwiching.

# ABOUT THE AUTHORS

**TAMI NOYES** is the author of *American Vegan Kitchen*. She lives, cooks, and blogs in her two-kitty home in Ohio. Besides her blog, www.veganappetite.com, Tami also contributes to several vegan sites. E-mail Tami at veganappetite@gmail.com.

**CELINE STEEN** is the coauthor of *500 Vegan Recipes*, *The Complete Guide to Vegan Food Substitutions*, and *Hearty Vegan Meals for Monster Appetites*. You can find her at www.havecakewilltravel.com and contact her at celine@havecakewilltravel.com.

# INDEX